Freshwater Fishing Secrets

MINNETONKA, MINNESOTA

FRESHWATER FISHING SECRETS

Printed in 2008.

Tom Carpenter
CREATIVE DIRECTOR

Dick Sternberg
EDITOR

Jen Weaverling
MANAGING EDITOR

Michele Teigen
SENIOR BOOK DEVELOPMENT COORDINATOR

Bill Lindner, Mike Hehner
PHOTOGRAPHY

David Schelitzche, Julie Cisler
DESIGNERS

13 14 15 / 13 12 11 10 09 08

© 1998 North American Fishing Club

ISBN 978-0-914697-85-5

North American Fishing Club
12301 Whitewater Drive
Minnetonka, MN 55343
www.fishingclub.com

CONTENTS

INTRODUCTION 3

BASS 4

   JERKIN' THE FLATS FOR LARGEMOUTHS *by Rick Taylor* 6

   NIGHT FISHING FOR SMALLMOUTHS *by Don Wirth* 12

   RIVER BASS ON TOP *by Rich Zaleski* 20

   THE LAST FRONTIER FOR GIANT STRIPERS *by Chris Altman* 26

PANFISH 32

   CRAPPIES: THE REST OF THE YEAR *by Rich Zaleski* 34

   ICING PANFISH – THE NEW TECHNOLOGY *by Dick Sternberg* 40

   ON THE TRAIL OF BULL 'GILLS *by Jack Gulnetti* 48

WALLEYE 54

   BIG-RIVER WALLEYES *by Chris Niskanen* 56

   EARLY-SEASON WALLEYES *by Dick Sternberg* 62

   JIGGING FOR HARDWATER WALLEYES *by Dick Sternberg* 68

   PLANING FOR WALLEYES *by Dave Mull* 72

   GIVE A RIP FOR WALLEYES *by Dick Sternberg* 80

   TURN WEEDS INTO WALLEYES *by James Churchill* 86

TROUT & SALMON 92

   VERTICAL "CASTING" FOR DEEP-WATER LAKERS *by Dick Sternberg* 94

   DEEP JIGGING FOR WINTER LAKERS *by Dick Sternberg* 100

   COPING WITH GREAT LAKES CURRENTS *by Tom Huggler* 106

   THE DROP-BACK TECHNIQUE FOR RIVER STEELHEAD *by Dave Richey* 112

PIKE & MUSKIE 118

   DEAD BAIT FOR WINTERTIME PIKE *by Dick Sternberg* 120

   MUSKIES AFTER DARK *by Dean Bortz* 124

   SUMMERTIME PIKE: THE COLDWATER CONNECTION *by Dick Sternberg* . .130

CATFISH 138

   FRESH BAITS FOR GIANT CATS *by Gerald Almy* 140

   JUGGIN' SUPENDED CATS *by Harry Ryan* 146

INDEX 152

Introduction

T hink of this book as your chance to jump in the boat with some of America's best anglers. Edited by Dick Sternberg, a former fisheries biologist who has built his reputation as a top angling educator, *Freshwater Fishing Secrets* highlights top techniques for taking everything from bass to walleyes, cats to stripers. If you read just one book this year, *Freshwater Fishing Secrets* should be that book!

Steve Pennaz

Executive Director
North American Fishing Club

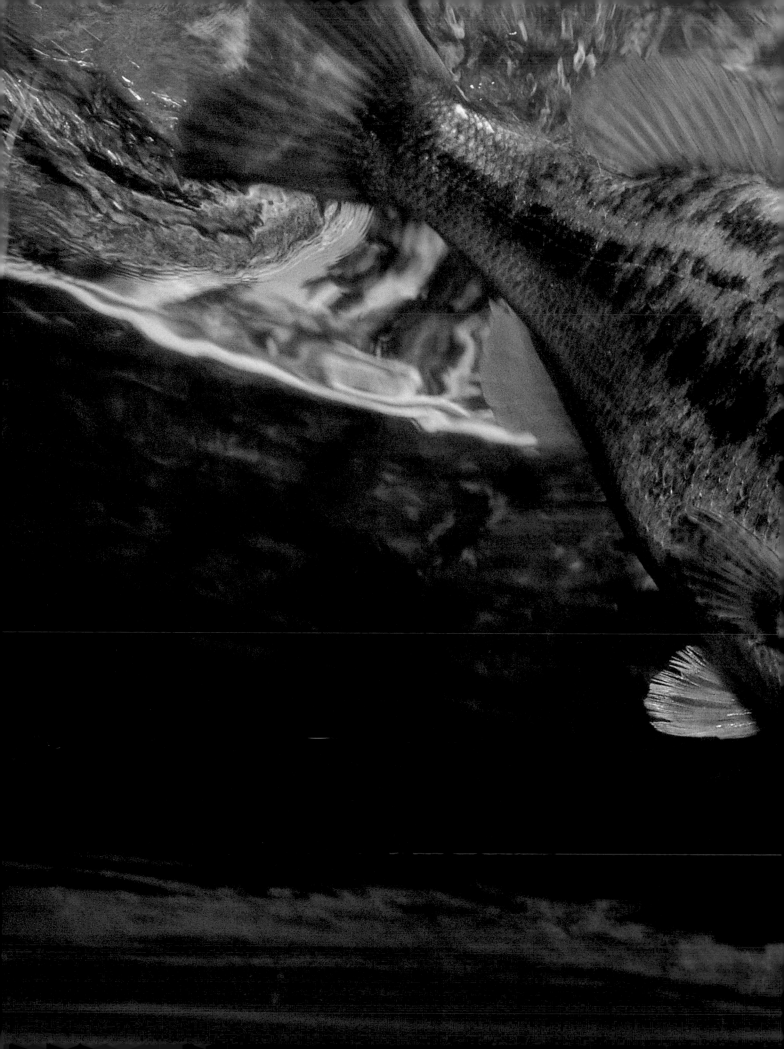

Bass

New break-throughs for America's favorite gamefish just keep on coming.

Jerkin' the Flats for Largemouths

by Rick Taylor

His 10-year-old heart was beating like a jack-hammer. Everywhere he looked he saw bass, nice keeper bass, wallowing just a few feet under the surface of the shallow, clearwater cove. Yet every lure he launched from the borrowed rowboat swam back unmolested.

Out of frustration, the die-hard youngster tied on a Rapala that sported three treble hooks. If the bass weren't going to bite, maybe he could at least snag one. He fired the lure downwind as far as possible and began jerking it back with all his strength.

A sudden thud telegraphed up his line and the water boiled. The excited kid fought the largemouth's every run and ploy, then eventually lifted it over the gunwale.

To his amazement, the 2-pounder was not snagged. It was solidly hooked in the mouth.

For the next hour, the lad hauled in bass after bass on virtually every cast. But it had to be the Rapala and it had to be ripped through the water with monster jerks. Attempts with other lures and techniques produced nothing.

More than three decades have passed since Larry Williams, while fishing the Lake James Chain in Indiana, accidentally discovered a method for putting inactive bass into the boat. Since then, that technique has proven to be a major factor in many of his fishing successes, including being a four-time qualifier for the BASS Masters Classic.

"It's kind of an ace-in-the-hole tactic that can help you out when nothing else is working," says Williams. "But it's most effective under a certain set of conditions."

"First, there needs to be a bright sun to warm the shallow water and bring up the bass. Next, you need some wind, because if the water is like glass, the bass will spook before you can get near them. Then all you need is a good, shallow flat and you're in business!"

Perhaps the real beauty of this technique is that it's well suited for that particular weather phenomenon notorious for sending anglers home with nothing more then a good excuse: the cold front. Warm air turns cold, water temperatures drop, the wind switches around to the north-northwest and cloudy or hazy skies become bright blue.

"Many people think this drives the bass deep and turns them off," says this part-time pro angler from Lakeview, Ohio. "While that may be the case for some fish, others will be looking for relatively warm water. And they'll find it in certain areas of the lake where the shallows are sun-baked and maybe sheltered a little from the wind!"

Jerkin' the flats works best on bright spring days with a little chop on the water.

When & Where to Jerk the Flats

In clear lakes, like the one he learned the technique on years ago, Williams has found that the best time for jerking minnowbaits is in the early spring . . . in fact, as early as just after ice-out. Apparently, the sun's warming rays better penetrate the water, soaking more quickly into the lake's bottom. In murky waters, sunshine gets absorbed in the first few feet, or even inches, of water.

In summer, however, clear-water bass are usually looking for cooler temperatures, not warmer, so they'll avoid the sunny flats. Interestingly enough, this is the time that jerking the flats works for Williams in muddier waters, such as the Ohio River, where he was once the Ohio points champion on the Redman tournament circuit. Flats are a major structure on those waters in summer, and Williams says the baitfish will come right up on them and get quite active, even with a hot sun and high water temperatures. The baitfish bring in the bass, and the bass bring Williams.

"Jerkin' the flats doesn't work all that well in the fall," says Williams. "Other tactics, like topwater fishing, are so effective that there's no sense wearing yourself out by jerkin'."

Another reason jerkin' doesn't work as well in fall is that the weather, the water temperature and the bass's desire to be in shallow water are all on a natural downhill trend. So, those sun-baked shallow flats, which are not warming all that much anyway, have lost some of their appeal.

Conversely, in spring, the bass, the water temperature and everything else are on their way up. Even if the main lake is only 40° F, a good shallow flat inside a cove can be as much as five degrees warmer. The best places to look for such coves are on the northern side of the lake. Since spring winds are predominantly from the south, they blow the sun-warmed, upper layer of the lake to northern areas. And, by facing south, these shorelines are also more open to direct warming from the sun.

"If you aren't familiar with the water," says Williams, "look at a good map and circle those areas where the contour lines are far apart. Ideally, the flat will be about 5 feet deep, but it can be as much as 15 feet, depending on water clarity. It will be on or near a north shore and have deep water nearby. In a man-made impoundment, that deep water is usually a submerged creek or river channel."

Williams explains that it's a bonus to have some kind of cover on the flat, even if it's only scattered. Weeds or brushpiles will better attract and hold both prey and predator. Still, cover is not mandatory; a bare flat may be just fine.

The slope of the flat is also relative. Williams prefers one that doesn't drop more than a few feet in a hundred yards. But again, it all depends on what the rest of the lake has to offer. As for size, he says a 30- to 40-acre flat is ideal, five acres is too small, and no flat can be too large.

A big flat (marked "1") is a prime spot for jerkin'.

Lures & Equipment For Jerkin'

Williams' first choice for jerkin' is a size 13 floating Rapala. His favorite color is black and silver, followed by black and gold, then blue and silver.

His second choice is the Bomber Long A, which has a gold or silver insert that causes a lot of flash and looks quite natural as it moves through the water. Being a little heavier, and with slightly more lip, the Bomber casts farther and runs a little deeper.

If even more distance or depth is required, Williams opts for the Bagley Bang-O-Lure in the same lengths and colors. And for those very deep flats, has found success with the Rebel Spoonbill, which gets down to 10 feet or more.

"Any number of rods and reels will work with this tactic," notes Williams. "I've always been partial to spinning outfits, so that's what I use. I like a 6½-footer with a fairly soft tip, because it helps cast those lightweight lures a long ways. If I'm working deeper flats, I'll go to a stiffer rod to help me get a better hookset." A long-spool spinning reel, filled with 8- to 10-pound mono, also helps make lengthy casts.

Williams attaches the bait with a Cross-Lok snap, rather than tying directly to the lure, because a snap gives the bait more wobble and also allows for faster lure changes.

WILLIAMS' FAVORITE
JERKIN' BAITS

(1) Size 13 Floating Rapala, (2) Bomber Long A, (3) Bagley Bang-O-Lure, (4) Rebel Spoonbill.

How to Jerk the Flats

"I usually start out near the shoreline," says Williams, who has been fishing professional tournaments since 1978. "I'll keep making passes and work my way out until I locate the main bass concentrations. It's hard to use a depth finder in shallow water, but if the bass are on a deeper flat, I may scout it with my electronics first."

A major key to the jerking tactic is to drift with the wind. If you're trying to follow a specific contour, use your trolling motor to stay on line. When a pass is completed, fire up the outboard, run back upwind and start over...perhaps 50 feet farther out this time. Unless the wind switches on you, it shouldn't be too difficult to keep each pass parallel to the others and thus thoroughly cover the flat.

You should also cast with the wind to help make your casts as long as possible. And since the wind will be blowing you toward your target, the length of your retrieve will be much shorter than your cast. Occasional angle

HOW TO JERK A MINNOWBAIT

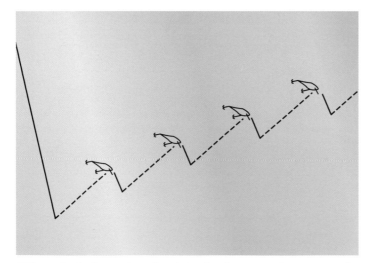

Start on the upwind side of the flat and cast downwind to maximize casting distance.

Start reeling as soon as the lure lands and make several sharp downward jerks with the rod to get the bait down to the desired depth.

When the bait reaches the right depth, pause for a second to allow it to float up. Give the bait several small twitches as it rises. Repeat the procedure all the way back to the boat.

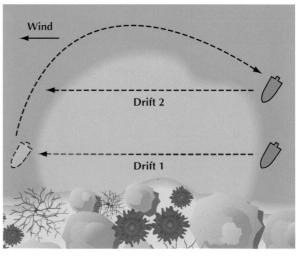

After completing the first drift, motor back to the upwind side, being careful not to run over the flat and spook the fish. Then, make another drift, about 50 feet farther out than the first one. Repeat until the entire flat has been covered.

casts are also recommended, wind permitting.

As soon as the lure splashes down, start reeling as fast as you can while jerking hard with rapid downward sweeps of the rod. The purpose here is to get the shallow-running lure down to its maximum depth immediately. Then, just stop for about one second and give five or six little twitches of the rod tip. This makes the lure quiver and, according to Williams, is what triggers most strikes.

If nothing hits, resume fast-cranking once again. Jerk hard a few times, then pause before applying the quiver. Keep this up all the way back to the boat.

"Basically, this is a numbers pattern, not a big bass pattern," Williams says. "You'll take a lot of bass in the 1- to 3-pound range. Big bass are lazy; they don't want to chase something that's shooting through the water, acting like a hard-to-catch baitfish."

When conditions are right, Williams jerks the flats to fill his limit, then goes after larger bass with other tactics. This has won him many club tournaments and placed him high in a number of national events.

"Your enemy when using this technique is flat water," Williams emphasizes. "You need a good chop on the surface. The only time a wind can get too strong is when it's riling up the water. Otherwise, if you can cast and keep the boat drifting in the right direction, you can effectively jerk a flat."

Williams recommends one more thing for jerking the flats: Conditioning. If you're not in fairly good shape, both mentally and physically, it may not be for you.

"It's a hard-work tactic that really tires you out," he says. But judging from Williams' success, jerking is one tactic that any fisherman who likes to catch large-mouths would do well to adopt.

Weighted Minnowbaits Trigger Negative Bass

When bass are lethargic, they may not want to chase a bait that is darting erratically and then rapidly floating up when it stops. Some innovative bass anglers have solved the problem by weighting their minnowbaits to make them neutrally buoyant. Once you jerk these baits down to the desired depth, you can work them much more slowly because they won't start to float up as soon as you start reeling.

This technique of hanging a weighted minnowbait right in the face of uninterested bass proved so deadly that some bait manufacturers started to produce pre-weighted minnowbaits. Today, practically every major minnowbait manufacturer makes some kind of suspending bait.

There is one problem with any neutrally buoyant bait: The buoyancy changes depending on the water temperature. The colder the water, the more weight you must add to make the bait neutrally buoyant.

Here is a technique for weighting your own minnow baits, or for fine-tuning pre-weighted baits.

Stick a piece of lead tubing on the front hook and trim it until the plug just sinks in a pan of water.

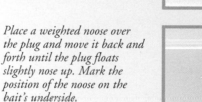

Place a weighted noose over the plug and move it back and forth until the plug floats slightly nose up. Mark the position of the noose on the bait's underside.

Drill a hole where you made the mark, add a little epoxy and push the lead into the hole.

File away the excess lead until the plug is neutrally buoyant (test it as you go) then seal the lead in with epoxy.

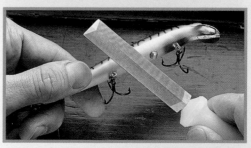

NIGHT FISHING FOR SMALLMOUTHS

by Don Wirth

In some parts of the country, particularly in the southeastern states, night fishing for smallmouth bass has assumed a cult status. Local anglers often fish from sundown to sunup, show up for work, then repeat the process the following evening. Surprisingly, in other parts of the country, night fishing is practiced only rarely.

After dark, big smallmouths go on the prowl, moving up from their deep-water haunts to feed in shallow water. Some experts feel these big smallies have two distinct feeding patterns during the summer months. By day, they feed on schooling forage fish that suspend near the thermocline, often 40 feet deep. By night, they move to banks, ledges, points, humps and weedbeds that harbor nocturnal crayfish. As the crawdads get active, so do the smallmouths.

On the Tennessee/Kentucky border sits scenic Dale Hollow Reservoir, a sprawling turquoise-colored impoundment noted for big smallmouth bass. Make that giant smallmouth bass. Dale Hollow gave up the world record smallie in 1955, an 11-pound, 15-ounce behemoth that some feel will never be equalled. Dale Hollow guide Fred McClintock, however, isn't a member of that group. He's convinced even bigger smallmouths swim in Dale Hollow, and he believes fishing at night is the best way to catch them.

McClintock has been a guide at Dale Hollow since 1985. A Pennsylvania native, he was originally attracted to the deep lake because of its legendary muskie fishing. But once he began fishing Dale Hollow for a living, he found that the allure of catching giant smallmouth bass was highly addictive. He soon became the most sought-after guide on the reservoir and has landed smallmouths approaching 8 pounds, muskies of more than 35 pounds and walleyes of more than 15. McClintock's fishing expertise has been featured frequently in major national fishing publications such as *North American Fisherman.*

"Night fishing for smallies is a whole different ball game – you either love it or you hate it," McClintock says. One way to learn to love it is to pre-plan your night fishing trip so you're not groping blindly for the right approach. "The two most common failures of anglers who try night fishing are not knowing what they're doing, and not knowing what to look for," McClintock notes. "Obviously, you can't concentrate on catching fish if you're lost. And, if you don't know the water, getting lost is a very easy thing to do."

McClintock recommends arriving at a new lake early in the afternoon and cruising potential fishing areas while you can still see where you're going. "Don't try to fish an entire lake or reservoir after dark, especially if you're new at night fishing," he advises. "Know the water you wish to cover, and work a confined area." He suggests studying a lake map to find a smaller area that has everything a fish needs for survival: a deep-water sanctuary, a shallow food shelf and a place to spawn.

"The right depth depends on the time of year and the water temperature. In early summer, the fish may be very shallow. Late in the summer, when the water gets hot, they may be extremely deep. Finding the right depth is more important than knowing what kind of jig they're hitting or what color pork rind works best."

Equipment & Lures

In deep, clear waters, daytime fishing involves mostly spinning gear and nearly invisible light line. Six-pound mono is standard for daytime fishing, with grubs and small hair jigs the most popular daytime baits. But this tackle may lead to trouble at night, McClintock believes. "There's really no good reason to use light tackle and wispy lines after dark – the name of the game is boating fish, not just getting strikes."

McClintock favors baitcasting tackle and 14-pound line for night fishing with spinnerbaits and heavy jigs, his two favorite nighttime lures. Most of his rods are 6 feet in length, and at least medium-heavy power. He uses heavy-power rods when fishing the heaviest (up to 1 ounce) spinnerbaits and jigs.

When fishing late in the summer, McClintock may use a longer baitcasting rod, up to 7 feet. He says that the longer sticks take up more line when you set the hook, increasing your odds of burying the hook point in the jaw of a smallmouth down 35 feet or more.

McClintock uses fluorescent mono, along with a black light. "Black lights have made night fishing much easier for the average angler, since they illuminate fluorescent lines and make them glow like neon tubing," he says. "They're especially critical when fishing jigs. A big smallmouth may inhale a falling jig and you'll never feel it. The black light makes even the slightest line movements show up so you can pop the hook into 'em quick."

A black light is a critical part of the night-fishing system

You need less tackle to fish after dark than during the day. "In fact, too many rods and reels only creates tangles and confusion," McClintock maintains. "I normally keep three rods pre-rigged with the lures I'm going to use, because changing lures is more trouble after dark. Snaps would make lure changing easier, but I don't recommend them for jigs and spinnerbaits."

All your tackle must be in perfect working order before hitting the lake at night. "We're after big smallmouths, so I don't want to take any chances with a malfunctioning drag or clashing gears," McClintock says. "It's well known among night fishermen that if anything can go wrong with your tackle, it will. Ever try to tear down a baitcasting reel in the dark? It's no fun at all!"

McClintock relies on only a few lures, all of which have single hooks. "Stay away from treble-hooked lures at night, with the possible

Keep three rods rigged with your favorite baits to avoid nighttime rigging woes.

exception of a topwater bait like a black Jitterbug," he recommends. "It's easier for big smallmouths to throw treble-hooked lures. They seem to get a lot more leverage against the hook. Use spinnerbaits, jigs and similar lead-bodied baits at night."

McClintock likes spinnerbaits for several reasons. "They vibrate when you retrieve them slowly, which may be more important to the fisherman than to the fish," he says. "I like to be able to feel my lure when I'm casting it into total darkness, and a spinnerbait feels like something's thumping on the end of my line."

"As the blades turn, they flash, reflecting any light from the moon, stars or surrounding man-made sources. That may not seem like much light, but remember that the best night fishing is in extremely clear water. On a moonlit night, I believe the fish can see even a slight reflection."

Early in the season, when the bass are relatively shallow, McClintock uses a 3/8-ounce spinnerbait with small blades. As the water warms and the fish go deeper, he stays with them by gradually increasing the weight. He has caught big smallmouths at depths exceeding 35 feet on 1-ounce spinnerbaits. "Not only is a heavy spinnerbait easier to get down, you'll be able to feel it and keep track of it," McClintock advises. "Plus, a heavier lure is easier to cast on a stout baitcasting rod. You'll backlash less than you would with a lighter lure, like a 1/4-ounce jig. That's important when you're out there in the dark."

McClintock prefers short-arm spinnerbaits because they "helicopter" better than long-arm models. He has good luck with willow-leaf blades, but he also uses Colorado and Indiana blades.

If the fish are striking short, McClintock adds a pork trailer, always a No. 11 Uncle Josh frog, staying with the general shade of the spinnerbait, but varying the color a bit. For example, if he's using a black spinnerbait, his usual choice during the dark of the moon, he may use a brown or purple pork frog; if he's using white, as he would on a moonlit night, he may add a chartreuse frog. McClintock believes this slight color contrast helps make the lures more visible in the dark.

(1) Tandem willow-leaf spinnerbait, (2) short-arm spinnerbait tipped with pork frog, (3) rubber-legged jig with crawworm trailer, (4) spider jig, (5) Jitterbug, (6) fly 'n rind.

Smallmouths love a jig tipped with a soft-plastic grub.

fishes a 3/8-ounce jig when the smallies are between 20 and 30 feet, and a 1/2-ouncer when they're deeper than 30. If the bass are on vertical structure, such as deep ledges, he uses a "drop" retrieve, letting the jig fall slowly on a tight line.

Hair jigs are a favorite of smallmouth night fishing addicts, but lately McClintock has had good success experimenting with a rubber-legged jig dressed with a soft plastic trailer, such as Hale's Craw Worm. This lure can be retrieved in short, erratic movements right across the bottom to simulate a live crayfish.

Another of McClintock's top picks is the spider jig. "These lures are known locally as 'creepy crawlies,' and they are deadly on lunker smallmouths at night," he says. McClintock's favorite spider jig is the Hoot-N-Ninny, manufactured by Zorro Baits. "This bait has a strong, sharp hook and a soft plastic trailer with twin twister tails," he explains. "There's a round, tentacled collar which fits behind the leadhead. This is perhaps the most critical design feature of this type of lure. When a smallmouth mouths the bait, it closes its jaws around that spongy collar and will very seldom blow out the lure, as often happens with a regular leadhead."

McClintock likes to fish spider jigs by dragging them slowly across the bottom to mimic a crayfish. On moonlit nights, he prefers sand, smoke, light green, red or chartreuse jigs. During the dark of the moon, he switches to black, purple, dark green or pumpkin.

"It doesn't take a big tacklebox to be an effective night fisherman," McClintock concludes. "A paper sack full of jigs and spinnerbaits and a couple of bottles of pork rind are all you really need."

Jigs are another important part of McClintock's night-fishing repertoire. "Here in Tennessee, we fish a lure known as a fly 'n rind," he explains. "It's basically just a hair jig with a pork rind trailer." Early in the season, McClintock sticks to lighter jigs, usually 1/4-ounce, with a U-2 or 101 pork trailer. He "swims" these lures at the edges of shallow flats. The swimming retrieve requires as long a cast as possible, then the lure is reeled slowly back to the boat with the rod at a constant 45-degree angle.

As the water heats up and the bass move deeper, McClintock goes to heavier jigs. He

Night-Fishing Techniques

McClintock has discovered certain night-fishing patterns that pay off time and again, and he's agreed to share them with NAFC members who are dedicated to catching bigger fish.

"Early in the season, when the surface temperature is barely bumping 80°F at Dale Hollow, I look for big, submerged weedbeds," he says. "Most smallmouth fishermen think the fish always hang around rocks, so the weeds are usually overlooked. You won't find weeds in many southeastern highland reservoirs, but when they're present, they will absolutely outdraw every other type of cover at the beginning of the night-fishing season."

Big weedbeds adjacent to smallmouth spawning flats can be found in midwestern mesotrophic lakes and Canadian shield lakes, as well as southern reservoirs. "When the spawn is complete, the fish hang around these flats for a few days, and then move out to the edges of the flats," McClintock observes. He has caught some of his biggest smallmouths at night in shallow weedbeds, often by running a big spinnerbait right over the weed tops.

Let's say you succeed in locating a good weedbed close to a spawning flat, but can't connect with fish. "Two things are happening: you're either fishing too deep, or the weedbed is not close enough to deep water," McClintock says. "Even though most of the bass are using shallow water, they like having deep water nearby—it gives them a sense of security."

Once the water warms and the weed pattern stops producing, McClintock shifts gears and begins seeking out deeper structure like ledges and drop-offs. Leadhead lures like the fly 'n rind or spider rig are the first choice now, although he also uses spinnerbaits.

"I have to slow down and fish at 20 feet or so," McClintock explains. "If there's a ledge or drop fairly close to a big spawning flat, particularly a big flat with weeds on it, that's the first place I'll look. Big smallmouths don't roam all over the lake—they're homebodies. I like to fish areas with a lot of good habitat in close proximity."

Besides drops and ledges, McClintock likes to fish deep points in hot weather. He doesn't hesitate to go as deep as 35 feet. "A point is a good bet in any deep body of water, especially

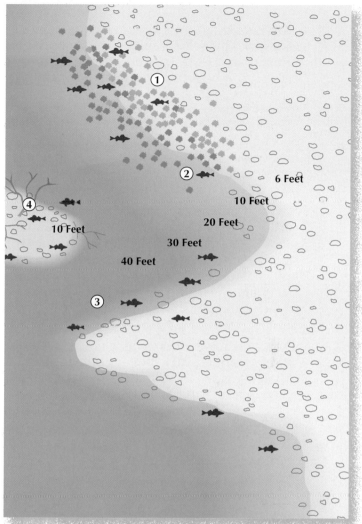

(1) A big weedbed near a spawning flat, (2) a drop-off along the edge of a weedy spawning flat, (3) a deep point that drops off sharply and (4) a hump surrounded by deep water.

at night," he says. "I like the points that drop sharply into deep water. Don't just fish the end, but cast to the deeper sides as well."

"Humps are probably the best structure I can think of for a truly giant smallmouths, simply because there's so much deep water surrounding them, and giant smallmouths really hang in deep water. Most fishermen pound the banks, so offshore humps stay unfished much of the time. If you can locate them, you're likely to have a great smallmouth spot that will produce all season, maybe for several seasons, if you don't take too many fish off it." McClintock's favorite humps have scattered stumps for cover. He normally fishes them at depths of 10 to 30 feet, relying mainly on a heavy spinnerbait.

How to Work A Spinnerbait

The way McClintock retrieves a spinnerbait varies with the season and depth. "A short-arm spinnerbait is especially effective at night because it can be dropped or helicoptered down ledges and drop-offs," he says. He casts the lure toward shallow water. Then, with the rod at a 45-degree angle, allows the spinnerbait to sink on a tight line. When it reaches the bottom, he lowers the rod tip, takes up slack with the reel and sweeps the rod back to 45 degrees. He repeats this motion until the lure reaches the boat.

When smallies are using shallower cover, such as a weedy spawning flat, McClintock often "slow-rolls" the spinnerbait. The lure is simply retrieved at a slow to moderate speed and kept just off the bottom or right over the top of the cover. The retrieve speed increases as the water gets shallower and decreases as it gets deeper.

To work a weedy spawning flat, just let the blades barely tick the tops of the weeds. "Then hang on," McClintock advises, " 'cause when that big girl comes blowing out of the grass, she's liable to jerk the rod clean out of your hands!"

Conservation Measures

Night fishing in hot summer weather has its upside, but there's a downside as well. "When the water surface temperature is in the 80°F to 90°F range, as is common in my area in summer, it's very hard on any smallmouths you carry in your livewell," McClintock points out. "I never put any fish in my livewell, except for a single trophy a client wishes to mount."

Local club tournaments held at night are especially deadly on the smallmouth population, he believes. "On the morning after a typical summer night tournament, you might spot 20 or 30 dead smallies floating around the dock where the fish were weighed in. This happens because the water was just too hot and the fish went into shock. If you must fish night tournaments or hold smallies in your livewell in hot weather, take the necessary precautions to keep them cool, and treat the livewell water with a catch-and-release compound, which calms the fish and slows their metabolism.

"Trophy fish are a precious resource – Take only what you need, and handle the rest with tender, loving care."

IMPORTANT SPINNERBAIT PRESENTATIONS

Let the spinnerbait helicopter down steep ledges, trees or other vertical cover.

Retrieve the spinnerbait with a lift-and-drop motion, raising it about a foot, letting it helicopter a little and then raising it again.

Reel a spinnerbait over the weeds, allowing it to brush the weed tops.

Slow-roll a spinnerbait across the bottom, allowing it to bump over brush piles, logs, rocks and other obstacles. Periodically lift it a foot or so and let it sink back to the bottom.

McClintock displays proof that night fishing works.

RIVER BASS ON TOP

by Rich Zaleski

"I'm not a topwater specialist per se," said Terry Baksay, keeping an eye on his plug drifting along the shoreline. As it reached an eddy created by a partially submerged log protruding from the riverbank, he brought it to life with a gentle twitch of the rodtip. "But when you find aggressive, object-oriented largemouths in shallow water, surface fishing can produce more and bigger fish." The words had hardly left Baksay's lips when his lure suddenly disappeared into a frothy boil. "Aggressive, shallow water bass," he grunted as he set the hook, "is what summertime river fishing is all about."

Baksay, of Easton, Connecticut, is a talented and confident tournament angler. He doesn't hesitate to cast into the face of conventional angling wisdom by relying on tactics like topwater fishing for river largemouths.

Conventional wisdom holds that the largemouth bass is a fish of still waters. But that belief has come up for review in recent years, as anglers across the country have found exceptional largemouth fishing in flowing rivers from the Saint John's in Florida to New York's Hudson and the Sacramento River of California. They're finding that largemouth bass inhabit rivers and moving water of all descriptions, including the upper reaches of impoundment tributaries. They're learning that largemouths in a river environment are rarely as severely turned off by unfavorable weather conditions as those in still water. And many are discovering an extraordinary connection between moving-water largemouth and topwater fishing.

"On big rivers," Baksay says, "fishermen have always looked to the quiet backwaters for largemouth bass. That theory holds up in the spring, and sometimes in the late fall. If there's real heavy weed growth in the back bays, some largemouths will use them all summer long. But in most river systems, plenty of largemouths will be out in the river during the summer and early fall."

Once you accept the idea that largemouths can and do thrive in current, tying on a surface lure is pretty much a common-sense strategy. Survival in the current requires more energy expenditure than life in still water. Since energy output requires fuel, it follows that river largemouths must feed more frequently than stillwater bass. To do so, they must feed more aggressively, a trait that should point the river bass angler toward shallow water, where most of the food is found.

Consistent largemouth catches are a matter of concentrating your efforts on the right spots in the right areas. It's easy to read water on a small stream, where differences in flow are visually evident among pools, riffles and runs. A big river has the same conditions, but on a bigger scale. The deeper and wider any particular stretch is, the slower the flow through that area, and the greater the chances of finding largemouths. Points or cuts in the bank, along with bars, wing dams and other sizable bank protrusions, alter the flow and further add to the attractiveness of an area. Within those areas, specific objects that break the current will determine the actual position of the bass.

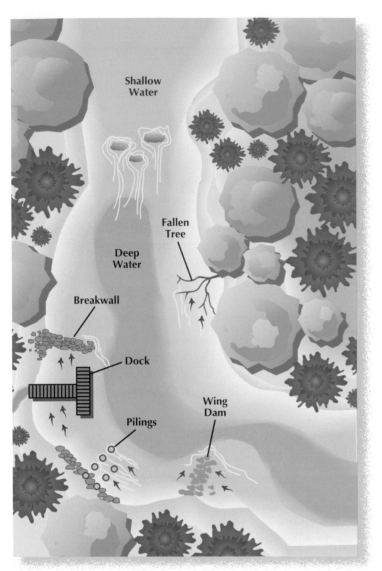

Prime locations for the drift-and-twitch method include fallen trees, breakwalls, docks, pilings, wing dams or any other objects that form a significant current break.

The Drift & Twitch Technique

Baksay finds river largemouths easy to locate and easy to catch, because they typically use areas of reduced flow and hold in eddies and slack-water pockets created by objects or cover. They let the current bring their meals to them, rather than hunting for food. In moving water a fish only gets one look at a meal before it passes downstream, so the fish soon learns to strike quickly. It's a perfect application for topwater tactics.

"The idea is to place your plug upstream of the object that's causing the current to shift directions," Baksay explains, "and let it wash into the fish's holding spot, just like natural food. I usually let it float free until just before it makes contact with the cover, then give it a twitch or a little movement of some kind. That's invariably when the fish will come out for it."

A surface plug drifting along aimlessly is easy for a bass to mistake for an injured or stunned baitfish, caught up in the current and unable to escape. A rod twitch to create the appearance of panic as it's swept into an area where the flow changes enhances the "believability" of the presentation. A bass has little choice but to react to it as something with a high probability of being an easy meal.

Baksay takes this line of reasoning one step further. "When I'm fishing shoreline objects," he says, "I like the plug to bump right against the shoreline as it's being washed downstream toward the log, bush, piling or whatever I'm fishing. I think that the natural tendency is for

HOW TO DRIFT A TOPWATER

Cast well upstream of the slack-water pocket where you suspect a bass is holding. Your cast should be no more than 30 feet in length.

Hold your rod tip high as the plug drifts, in order to keep the line off the water and prevent the current from causing too much drag.

creatures caught up in the current to struggle toward the shoreline in an attempt to get out of it. That's what I try to make my plug look like it's doing."

The object of the game is to let the natural flow of the current direct your lure to some type of object or cover. Once you fool that fish into grabbing your offering, you've got to get it out of and away from the cover in a hurry, and the first few feet of the battle are critical. This is an application that requires fairly heavy tackle. Because of the nature of the presentation though, thick line can interfere with the lure's ability to look natural.

"In some ways," says Baksay, "it's like fly fishing, because you have to be aware of the current drag on your line. Too much line lying out in the heavier current, away from the bank, will pull the lure away from shore and cause it to speed up. It'll blow by the object the fish is holding behind, instead of lingering there or bumping against it. The heavier the line, the more likely this will happen."

"But you need fairly heavy line for the kinds of cover that largemouths use in heavy current – typically about 14- or 17-pound test. My solution is using a long rod, limiting my casts to 25 or 30 feet and holding the rodtip high. This keeps most of the line off the water as the lure floats with the current."

Lure placement and boat position are important aspects of Baksay's short-cast/high-rod technique. The nose of his boat is always pointed upstream, and he tries to get into ideal position before making a cast toward an object he suspects might hold a bass. "A lot of fishermen hurry too much and, as soon as they finish fishing one log, they make a cast upstream, past the next object. Nine times out of ten, the fish will hit on the first cast if the lure approaches it properly. But if it blows past a couple of times or, worse yet, if you get it hung on the cover and have to go in and un-snag it, the fish will be gone or totally spooked by the time you get in position to present the bait properly."

Instead of casting anxiously as soon as you spot a potential lie, Baksay suggests investing the time to position yourself in the ideal spot and make the first cast count. You'll make fewer casts during the day, but more of them will properly expose your lure to bass that are ready to bite.

Baksay keeps his boat 15 to 20 feet off the cover or the bank and casts to the shoreline. He aims his cast 10 to 15 feet upstream of the target, from a position just slightly upstream of the eddy formed by the object. Keeping the rodtip high, he takes up excess line as the lure floats into position. When it reaches the high-percentage spot where he expects the strike to occur, the plug is slightly downstream of his rodtip. Any twitch of the rod will now cause the lure to hesitate in that spot and usually to turn, often drawing a reaction strike from the bass. When he sets the hook, he's already pulling the fish away from the cover, not into it, through it or across it, as he would if his boat were downstream of the cover.

Unless he has some specific reason to suspect that a particular piece of cover is holding a fish, Baksay won't often make more than

Twitch the bait slightly just as it reaches the slack-water pocket. It will hesitate and turn, imitating an injured baitfish making a last-ditch attempt to escape.

Set the hook when you feel the weight of the fish. Pull the fish away from the pocket so it can't get tangled in the cover.

two or three casts before moving his boat into position to work the next object upstream. "Of course," he cautions, "a lot of the objects you're fishing are pretty complex, like fallen trees, multiple pilings and so forth. You have to treat each limb, rock or whatever, as a separate break, and you may only move the boat a few feet to get the right drift for the next target. But in a good bass river, there are plenty of targets, so don't waste too much time on one tree or rock pile if it doesn't produce something quickly."

"If you do catch a fish though, back off long enough to correct your position and fish the break again. River bass are often loners, but they may travel in small packs or larger schools."

The rod you choose for this style of fishing is important, because it has to perform several specific tasks. Baksay's choice is a 7-foot, medium-heavy-power graphite baitcasting rod that can handle a wide variety of lure weights. This rod will make accurate casts, yet is stiff

enough to pull fish out of the tangle as soon as you set the hook. And it's long enough to keep most of the line off the water as the plug drifts.

Since the fishing is almost entirely visual, sensitivity isn't much of a consideration. Neither is the rod's action. You're not so much retrieving the lure as picking up slack as it floats downstream, twitching it a few times, at most, on each cast.

The importance of a rod that can handle a wide range of lure weights becomes apparent when you consider Baksay's standard arsenal of river topwaters. The Zara Spook he uses weighs almost 3/4 ounce – the size 11 Rapala he prefers in clear water, less than 1/4 ounce.

Between those extremes are the Slug-Go, a soft stickbait; a propbait; and a heavier minnowbait, a size 11 Magnum Rapala.

The Slug-Go has an erratic action and is much more snag-resistant than treble-hooked hard stickbaits. The propbait comes into play in situations where the plug can drift behind

BAKSAY'S FAVORITE TOPWATERS

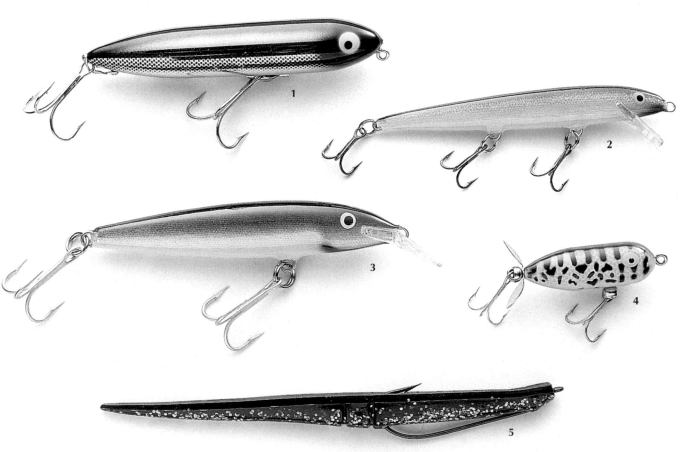

(1) Zara Spook, (2) size 11 Floating Rapala, (3) size 11 Magnum Rapala, (4) Tiny Torpedo, (5) Slug-Go.

pilings or tree limbs. "If I can get the plug into a tight spot like that and stop it with the line," says Baksay, "the current will work the propeller while the plug is just bobbing around, and that seems to really trigger bass. Getting them back out the opening the plug floated through can be a problem, but I'd rather deal with that than not get the fish on at all."

The slight diving action of the Rapala is often the most effective trigger. The bait floats along lifelessly and, just as it reaches the eddy, it turns and dips beneath the surface a few inches. It then floats back up like a crippled baitfish struggling to escape the predator it knows is lying in wait nearby. The lighter Rapala is superb in clear water, but it may not present a substantial enough target or create enough of a disturbance to be noticed in roiled water. That's where the heavier Magnum version comes into play.

While he utilizes variations in lure action to trigger fish, Baksay doesn't put too much stock in some other commonly held beliefs about what causes fish to strike a lure. He believes, for instance, that lure color is only minimally important in this kind of fishing.

"The fish only gets a glimpse of the bait anyway, and the distortion caused by moving water helps camouflage it," Baksay says. "I experiment with a variety of colors but mostly I like anything that looks like a minnow or shad, your basic white or chrome belly and a darker back. My next choices would be all black for very dark or very bright sky conditions, and something chartreuse for muddy water. You need that chartreuse in dingy water, and a lot of the best largemouth rivers are pretty muddy."

"Once you've learned to recognize the probable strike zone, let the current propel the plug and use the rod to guide it into position. Getting the fish to come up and take a shot at a lure usually isn't much of a problem if you're anywhere near right with the color. Getting a hook in them can be a problem, though, at least until you've got the moves down. Always let the fish take the plug under before you set the hook. With the lure that close to the tip of that long, stiff rod, missed hooksets can be dangerous. You won't miss many if you use super-sharp hooks and let the fish turn back toward its hideout with the plug in its mouth. There's a fine line between setting too early and waiting so long that the fish drags your plug too far back into the cover."

This nice bass fell for Baksay's drift-and-twitch method.

To ensure a hookup, Baksay replaces any plated hooks or beak-style trebles that come on plugs from the factory with short-shank, light-wire, "perfect-bend" bronze trebles. He attaches the new trebles with split rings, even if the factory hooks weren't so installed. He sharpens each point of each treble before using the plug, and touches them up with a hook hone at regular intervals during the day. They must be sharp enough to catch on contact, so the plug "sticks" in the fish's mouth before you set.

Regardless of where you live, there's probably a sizable river not too far away. And odds are, it harbors largemouth bass. During the summer it's a good bet that those bass are ready and willing to take a surface bait. You may have to ignore conventional angling wisdom to get up the confidence to give it a try, but the fun and excitement are more than worth the time it takes to find out.

THE LAST FRONTIER FOR GIANT STRIPERS

by Chris Altman

One look at a striped bass tells you it is a fish engineered for a life in moving water. Its long, torpedo-shaped body is designed to slice through the flow, while its heavy musculature and broad tail provide the power necessary to overcome the strongest currents. At sea, stripers must cope with tides and they ascend many miles up freshwater streams to deposit their eggs in moving water.

Arthur Kelso Jr., a high school teacher from Loudon, Tennessee, began fishing for river stripers in 1975. Watts Bar Lake had been stocked with the saltwater transplants, and the tailrace below Fort Loudon dam upstream from Watts Bar was (and still is) a popular hangout for striper enthusiasts. "I fished for stripers there for several years but couldn't catch any over 25 pounds," Kelso says. "Most of the fish I caught were 10 or 12 pounds. I knew there were bigger fish around, so I began doing a little detective work."

"I talked with a few fisheries biologists and one of them said that there may not be enough oxygen in the tailwater area to support the bigger fish. He suggested that I go downstream about two or three miles." The water in the tailrace is pulled from the lake bottom and has a very low dissolved-oxygen content, especially in summer. The downstream reaches should hold more oxygen because of contact with the air and the mixing action of the current.

Dave Bishop, Assistant Regional Manager for the Tennessee Wildlife Resources Agency and a recognized striped-bass expert, agrees that a few dams may have an oxygen problem that limits striper activity in the tailrace area. "But in most instances, I think that the reason tailwaters don't produce larger stripers has to do with the fish's nature rather than any kind of oxygen problem," he said. "It might be that larger fish don't like to fight the strong tailrace current, although I have no concrete data to back that up."

Whatever the problem was, Kelso was not finding the monstrous stripers he was searching for, so he decided to check out some downstream waters. "I had no idea where to look," he said, "so I started drifting big shad though likely-looking runs. While fishing along a particular island, I hooked 12 fish in 12 drifts, and nine of them broke my line. I knew I was on to something."

Kelso continued to experiment, developing a very successful system for fishing rivers. How successful? His average fish weighs 20 to 25 pounds, and his largest river striper to date is a 47-pound giant! News of his tremendous success spread rapidly, and he is now considered one of the area's top striper fishermen.

Despite the fact that striped bass are at home in current, most anglers overlook rivers and streams when hunting trophy stripers, preferring instead to work the still waters of reservoirs. And the anglers that do opt to fish rivers usually spend their time in the popular tailrace areas below the dams. But rivers often hold striper populations that are virtually untapped. These river-run stripers are the last frontier of striped-bass angling.

Where to Find River Stripers

Bridge piers are the most obvious current breaks in many rivers. Stripers may hold upstream, downstream or alongside a pier.

"Think shallow for river stripers," Kelso advises. "When the fish get hungry, they move into shallow water. From spring through mid-summer, most of my fish are caught in water less than 10 feet deep, and I catch a lot of them in only 2 or 3 feet."

But in late summer and fall, you'll find the biggest stripers in deeper parts of the river. "I look for a 25- to 35-foot hole," Kelso says, "especially one that has a sunken tree. There may be only one striper per spot, but it will be a big, dominant fish."

Kelso recommends targeting current breaks. As you move downstream, watch for any kind of surface boil, which indicates a below-water obstruction that is breaking the flow and creating surface turbulence. It might be a big rock pile, a stump or an old car; it makes no difference. The key is that the structure is located in relatively shallow water and that it breaks the current.

"When you see a boil, go back upstream, shut off your big motor and drift over the boil while watching your depth finder," Kelso suggests. "What you are looking for is a change in depth. The water might go from 15 feet to 7

Prime River Striper Habitat

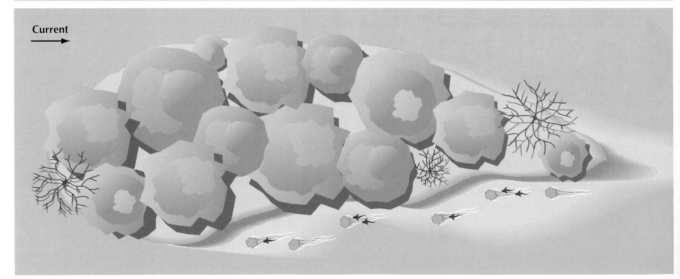

Submerged stumps along the fringes of islands are favorite hangouts for giant stripers. Large eddies form behind the stumps, making excellent resting spots and ambush points for stripers.

then back to 15 feet once you pass over the top of the object. This is a feeding area, and sooner or later a striper will show up. And when it does, it's going to hit your bait because it's there for the sole purpose of feeding. If it wasn't hungry, it would be in deep water."

"Bridge piers (pilings or abutments) are one of the most productive spots in any river. The pilings break the current and there is usually a lot of construction debris remaining on the bottom. That debris and the eddies around the pilings attract baitfish and the stripers follow. You know exactly where the fish will be."

"I usually start at the first pier that is in shallow water and close to the river channel. The pilings are usually set at an angle to the current flow, so one side of the pier will have more current than the other. Without fail, the fish will be on the side with the strongest current. They might be on the upstream side of the pier, in the eddy just downstream or in the swift water alongside it. Whatever their location, you can be certain that they will be facing into the swift current."

"Once I've determined which side of the pier has the swiftest current," he continued, "I motor upstream, cut the outboard and begin my drift." Kelso uses his electric trolling motor to keep the boat on course.

"You want the boat to pass within a few feet of the pier," he points out. "But never let the boat bump it or you'll spook every striper in the area! Bridges usually hold a lot of fish, so be sure to fish them thoroughly before you leave."

Another of Kelso's favorite striper hangouts is a row of stumps on an island. "If the river you are fishing is affected by a dam, and most are," he says, "trees along the island's outside edges were more than likely cut so they would not endanger boat traffic. This left a row of underwater stumps that makes an ideal feeding area for stripers, especially for really big ones. For that reason, I work my way completely around an island, trying to hit every single stump I can locate. I've found that stripers tend to hold tighter to stumps than they do to any other object, so you have to make sure you get your bait right up against them. Most of my biggest fish have come from these stump rows. In fact, if I was going strictly for a big striper, that's the only place I'd fish."

"As the lake downstream from the river warms up, fishing in the river gets better and better. Stripers prefer cool water, and the river stays quite a bit cooler than the main lake. The current also draws stripers. This puts a tremendous number of fish in a smaller, relatively confined area, and that makes for some great fishing!"

"My experience has shown that the most productive months for taking river stripers are July, August and September. After that, the fishing gradually tapers off, because most of the fish move back to the lake."

Boils in midriver indicate the presence of a rock pile or other structure that breaks the current. Stripers often hold in the downstream eddy.

Deep holes, especially those with sunken trees, hold the biggest stripers in late summer and fall.

Threadfin shad are easy to distinguish from gizzard shad by the longer filament on the dorsal fin and the yellowish, rather than blackish, margin on the tail. Skipjack do not have a filament on the dorsal fin.

Bait & Tackle

Kelso insists on healthy, live bait. "One of my favorites is a 5- or 6-inch yellowtail (threadfin) shad," he says, "but they can be very difficult to catch. Most of the time, I use 6- to 8-inch gizzard shad. But when I'm after huge fish, I'll switch to 2- or 3-pound river herring (skipjack)."

When using a long-handled dip net to catch shad, Kelso intentionally dips only two or three at a time to avoid damaging them. When cast netting, he tosses the net to the outer fringe of the shad school for the same reason.

"Pick out only the strongest, healthiest-looking bait," Kelso advises, "and don't crowd them in the bait tank. As a general rule, I carry one shad for each gallon of water in the tank. Really big shad require two gallons each."

Kelso's tackle consists of a 7- to 8-foot, medium-heavy power baitcasting rod with a fairly light tip. A sturdy level-wind reel with a clicker allows the fish to take the bait without feeling much resistance.

"I use 25- to 30-pound mono, because the water is usually murky and I don't have to worry about it spooking the fish," he explains. "I need the strongest line I can get away with to land big fish in the rough structure. I tie a new knot after every fish I catch, and I strip off 2 to 3 feet of line every time."

Kelso's terminal gear is quite simple. He makes a slip-sinker rig by sliding a 1-ounce egg sinker onto the line, tying on a hook and then pinching on a split shot about 18 inches up the line to serve as a stop. "In spring, when I'm using smaller shad, I'll go with a straight size 3/0 Eagle Claw hook," he says. "But the shad get bigger as the season progresses, so I use bigger shad for bait. Then, I'll go with a 5/0 hook. I run the hook through the mouth and out the upper jaw. When I'm using big river herring, I switch to a 10/0 shark hook, but I usually use these without a weight. I file all of my hooks to a razor point."

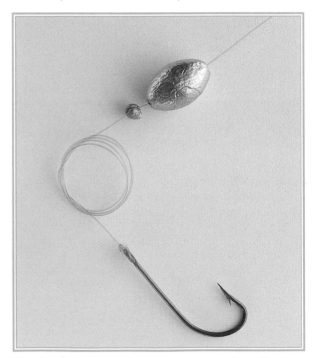

The basic live-bait rig for stripers consists of a 1-ounce egg sinker and a size 3/0 to 5/0 hook. A split shot acts as a stop. Push the hook into the mouth and out the upper jaw.

Techniques for River Stripers

When drifting, it's important to keep quiet. Stripers are skittish by nature, and when they are just under your boat, nearly any noise will spook them. Never use an outboard motor around an area that might hold a fish; instead, use your electric, but use it sparingly. Don't slam a storage compartment lid, stomp or bang around in the boat or talk any more than is absolutely necessary.

"Sometimes, the fish will spook just from the boat floating over the them," Kelso says, "so you want your bait to be the first thing they see. That's why I always fish from the front of the boat. With an 8-foot rod, I can keep my bait 8 or 10 feet ahead of the boat. By the time the boat passes over the fish, it has already hit my shad.

"When I'm fishing the stumps, I like to free-line a big herring and let it swim where it wants to while I drift. I believe a trophy striper, even when it's not hungry, will hit a herring. I might not get more than a single hit in two or three days of fishing, but when a fish takes a 3-pound herring, you know it's a trophy!"

When he hooks a fish, Kelso continues drifting with the current until he lands it. Then, he motors back upstream and drifts the spot again. It's not unusual for him to catch two or three fish off the same small piece of structure.

Another technique that's starting to catch on is topwater fishing. "Works best in May, when the water gets up to 60 degrees," Kelso says. "In early morning or late evening, I cast a Cordell Redfin up into 2 or 3 feet of water along the banks of islands and reel it just under the surface so it makes a 'V.' Drives stripers mad."

River fishing for giant stripers is starting to catch on across the South. In Kentucky's Cumberland River, for instance, stripers are growing to mammoth size on a trout diet, with several fish over 50 pounds being reported.

Kelso tells a story about a good 'ol boy who was hunting in a tree stand alongside the river when he saw what he thought was a huge carp on a shallow gravel bar. "He drew a bead on the fish and practically blew its head off. But when he dragged it up on the bank, he saw it was a giant striper. He loaded it the back of his pick-up, took it home and put it on the hog scale. It reportedly weighed over 60 pounds – without its head!"

A long rod, 7 to 8 feet in length, enables you to keep the bait drifting ahead of the boat.

Cast a shallow-running minnowbait up to the bank and retrieve slowly so the lure stays just beneath the surface and makes a noticeable wake.

Panfish

Millions of anglers are discovering that these scrappy fighters are not just for kids.

CRAPPIES: THE REST OF THE YEAR

by Rich Zaleski

In spring, everybody is a crappie expert. That's because pre-spawn crappies are almost suicidal. But experts are a lot harder to find in late June, and by August they are few and far between.

Doug Eriquez is one of the few experts that specialize in catching crappies the rest of the year. The only time he doesn't do much crappie fishing is in spring, when the shallows are teeming with the speckled fish. "I'm busy fishing bass tournaments in May and June," he says, "and there are too many fishermen pounding on the crappies anyway. I wait until summer and fall to catch mine. It's nothing like spring fishing, but it can be very good."

According to Eriquez, the reason anglers have trouble catching crappies in summer is that they fish for them in the same shallow cover where they found them in spring. "Summer crappies," he explains, "use cover, but only to rest in. When they're feeding, they're on the move in open water."

"And even when they do use cover, it's not the shallow bushes and weeds they're around in May. Summer crappies use deep weed edges and fallen trees that reach into deep water. Standing timber can also be good, but it's not too common around here."

"Around here" for Eriquez is the northeastern part of the country. He lives in New Milford, Connecticut, and spends some of his time fishing large man-made lakes. But he especially enjoys fishing for crappies in smaller natural lakes.

Deep cover is hard to find in these glacially formed bodies of water, making it difficult to locate fish. On the following pages, Eriquez describes his system for finding open-water crappies in natural lakes.

Eriquez chooses to do the bulk of his crappie fishing in smaller, natural lakes.

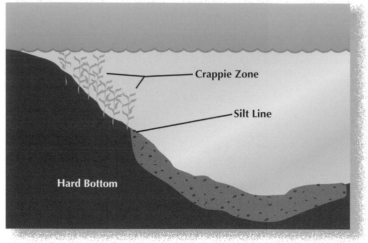

Look for crappies from the edge of weeds that reach the surface to the "silt line," where the bottom turns soft.

Finding Crappies in Summer

"Even when they're in open water, crappies relate to something," Eriquez maintains. "I always try to figure out what they're focusing on, but sometimes it's impossible."

Eriquez believes that crappies relate to such things as the edge of the hard-bottomed shoreline shelf, the edge of the weeds, a water-color break or a school of baitfish. The baitfish follow the plankton, which is moved by current and wind and changes depth according to how much sunlight there is. It may look like crappies are wandering aimlessly, but they're really following their food.

Since plankton – the primary link in the food chain – is thickest on the downwind side of a lake, that's where Eriquez begins his

search. He relies heavily on his flasher to pinpoint where crappies are holding. "I just wander back and forth from the deep basin to the shallows, with the gain cranked way up so I have a second echo," he says. "The location where the bottom signal weakens and the second echo disappears is the silt line. There, the bottom composition changes from hard to soft. From that edge to the edge of shallow-water weeds that reach the surface is the crappie zone. If the weeds end in a wall right at the drop-off, I look for someplace where there's an extension of the flat beyond the weeds, like a point or bar."

On a good crappie lake, you'll see fish blips on the screen while you're doing your reconnaissance work. Eriquez believes it's a mistake to stop and fish every time you see a suspended fish or two. You might catch a handful of crappies that way, but they're going to move and you'll have no idea where. "I like to get the 'lay of the land' first to find out what the fish are relating to," he explains.

"If I see a big bunch of fish, I might stop and try fishing. But usually I just toss a marker buoy near the school. When I'm zig-zagging along a drop-off, I may see two or three big groups of fish within a quarter mile, and I'll drop a marker on each one. Then I look at the pattern of my marker buoys. Often, I find that I'm marking the same school; the markers tell me how the fish are moving and help me figure out what they're relating to."

If Eriquez doesn't see any schools of fish worth marking, he concentrates on making a mental picture of the structure while noting scattered, individual fish blips. This gives him

HOW TO FIND CRAPPIES IN SUMMER

Watch your depth finder for blips well off bottom. If you find a lot of blips in a narrow depth range, that's where you want to fish.

Drop a marker buoy when you find a school, and then track the school's movement by dropping additional buoys.

When you lose the school, troll around in an oval-shaped path as shown, casting your jig and watching the flasher until you find the fish again.

an idea of the depth range of the fish and how far from the breakline they're holding.

"Ignore any fish that appear real shallow or real close to bottom, and the ones that are within a few feet of the weed edge," he suggests. "They're probably not crappies. Most crappies will stay in a pretty narrow depth band... say, from 12 to 17 feet, or 15 to 18 feet. That's the depth you want to fish."

"Develop a mental image of how the bulk of the blips within that depth range were positioned. Over the drop-off? Along the edge of the basin? Fifty feet or so from the weedline? Look for a common pattern, and don't worry about a few exceptions. You're concerned with what the biggest bunches of fish are doing, not a few stragglers."

Because he's convinced that crappies are mobile, Eriquez only anchors on exceptionally windy days. More often, he uses the electric motor to hold himself in the area of a school. By backing the boat into the wind, with the transom-mounted electric motor on a low speed setting, he hovers in place over or alongside the school.

Since you're dealing with crappies that are on the move, it may be difficult to stay in contact with the school. The quicker you can figure out which direction they are moving, the faster you can regain contact when they move out of range. When Eriquez loses the fish, as evidenced by four or five casts without a hit, he makes loose, ever-expanding oval passes around the spot he last saw them, with the long side of the ovals running parallel to the breakline.

It may take a few minutes to regain contact with the school, but once he catches one or sees the school on his flasher, he has a good idea of the direction in which they're moving. From then on, he tries to slide the boat along the breakline with the fish, keeping the transom pointed roughly into the wind.

Keeping your lure at the right depth is critical with this technique. If you are not getting bites, you need to know if the school has vacated the area or if you're working too far above or beneath the fish. As a rule, you should work the upper half of the depth range that you believe the crappies are using. "They'll come up for a bait," Eriquez says, "but they won't go down. A foot under the fish, and you've missed them. But you can be three feet over them and still get bites."

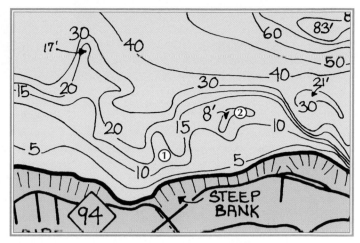

Sharp turns in the weedline (1) and an 8-foot hump (2) make ideal fall crappie locations.

Finding Crappies in Fall

As the water cools in fall, crappie don't move shallower right away. The first change in their behavior is to spend more time each day resting along breaks than moving. The movement patterns are similar to those in summer, but the fish will usually be closer to the breakline, and when they encounter something like a fairly sharp turn in the weed edge, a rocky hump or a deep patch of green vegetation, they are likely to hang around it for a while.

In some lakes, there is a period in the fall when crappies move back into shallow cover... usually just after the surface matted vegetation starts to fall back from summer levels. "The weed die-off evidently exposes a lot of prey," Eriquez theorizes. "When the water temperature drops down to about 55°F or so, the crappies head right back to where they were during the spawn, but not quite as deep. It's a lot like spring fishing, because you're casting jigs at shallow cover."

That shallow movement only lasts a few weeks and, in some lakes, might not happen at all. Once it's passed, the fish move back out to the open water, often settling in areas much deeper than those they used in summer. "In later fall, the crappies don't move as much," says Eriquez. "They tend to hold around deeper cover – sometimes as deep as 40 feet. They'll change depth, moving almost straight up over the cover they're holding on, and they could be 15 feet down over 50 feet of water. The next day, they could be 35 feet down, but they're still in the same spots, at least until the ice starts to form."

A chenille-and-marabou jig is hard to beat for slab crappies.

Equipment, Lures & How to Fish Them

On the small natural lakes where Eriquez does much of his fishing, he finds a cartop boat with an electric motor and a flasher more than sufficient. On the bigger impoundments, he uses a bass boat for crappie fishing.

"Ninety percent of the time, I use a ⅛-ounce jig. I know that it sinks a little less than a foot per count, and I know how fast to work it to keep it moving more or less horizontally," he says. "Sometimes, they won't hit something sinking that fast though, so you'll have to go to a ¹⁄₁₆-ounce. I find it tougher to gauge the depth of a lighter jig, and the wind can affect it too much, so if I can possibly catch 'em on an a ⅛-ounce, I feel a lot more confident."

"I use plain, old-fashioned, chenille-and-marabou crappie jigs almost exclusively. And if I have yellow, white and black, I'm all set." Actually, he uses yellow jigs almost all the time, and only tries black or white if the fish aren't responding. Plastic curlytails, tube-style jigs and plastic-bodied, marabou-tailed jigs all catch crappie. But Eriquez believes the chenille-and-marabou jig works as well as anything, so why confuse the issue with additional choices?

"The more different jig styles and color combinations you have in your box, the more time you spend second-guessing yourself and tying on new lures," he warns. "The answer to catching them is locating them, not trying to turn them on with some fancy color."

There is one other lure that Eriquez uses for crappies – a size 3 Jigging Rapala, which is normally considered an ice-fishing lure. He relies on the Rapala more in fall than in summer. "The fish move so steadily in the summer that it's tough to get right on top of them long enough to fish vertically," he explains. "In fall, when they settle down more, you can drop it right down to them."

Eriquez has found that the Rapala works best if he holds it motionless in the water. "I've had them nail it while the rod was resting on the gunwale," he says, "but, usually, I'll lift it a foot or so, hold it there for a few seconds, and then drop it back very slowly. Then I'll let it sit for a minute before repeating the action. If you jig it steadily the way you do when ice fishing for trout or perch, you won't get many crappies."

You can catch crappies through the summer and fall if you adopt Doug Eriquez's theories and methods. Combine them with what you already know about springtime crappie fishing, and you're in business for the entire open-water season.

ERIQUEZ'S FAVORITE CRAPPIE BAITS

(1) Chenille-marabou jig, (2) curlytail jig, (3) tube jig, (4) Fuzz-E-Grub, (5) size 3 Jigging Rapala.

CRAPPIE-FISHING TIPS

Attach the jig with a clinch knot and position the knot so the jig hangs horizontally. Always reposition the knot after you catch a fish.

Keep your lure just above the level where you see the fish. A crappie is much more likely to come up for a bait than go down for it.

Icing panfish — The new technology

by Dick Sternberg

A thin red band moves around the flasher dial as the ice fisherman lowers his tiny ice fly into the depths. The band dances up and down as the fisherman begins jigging.

Suddenly, a second red band appears on the flasher dial, just below the first. A crappie has spotted the lure and moved in for a closer look. As the angler continues jigging, the lower band remains stationary; the crappie is not interested enough to strike. But when the fisherman begins raising the lure and jigging it rapidly, the fish responds. The lower band grows wider, its color becomes more intense and it begins moving upward.

As the gap between the top and bottom bands close, the fisherman prepares for a strike. The rod tip twitches, he instantly sets the hook and begins to reel in the fish.

Before ice fishermen had these sensitive "underwater eyes," catching panfish or any other fish through the ice was a lot more difficult. If you weren't catching fish, you never knew if you were in the wrong spot or if the fish just weren't biting. Sometimes you would move to a different spot when there were plenty of fish right beneath your feet. Other times, you failed to catch the fish that were there because you were fishing at the wrong depth or working your lure the wrong way.

With good electronics, you know when you're on fish and when you're not, and you can adjust your presentation to entice them to bite.

Besides ultra-sensitive sonar devices, anglers are taking advantage of many other technological breakthroughs – better tackle, better line, better augers and better ice shelters – to help them pull more fish through holes in the ice. Here are the latest techniques and best equipment for my favorite wintertime quarry: crappies, bluegills and yellow perch.

A sensitive flasher is a big help in catching winter crappies.

Crappies

Crappies are the nomads of the freshwater gamefish. Although there are times when they concentrate along a drop-off or among the branches of a submerged tree, they're just as likely to suspend in the middle depths, far from any kind of structure or cover. And there's no guarantee that a spot where you find a big school one day will hold a single fish the next. Because finding them can be so difficult, location should be your main concern.

When the ice first forms, crappie fishing is easy. Chances are they will be in shallow, weedy bays – often the same bays that draw fish in early spring. But after a couple weeks or so, the fish begin to filter out of the bays and move into deeper water. That's when locating and catching them becomes much harder.

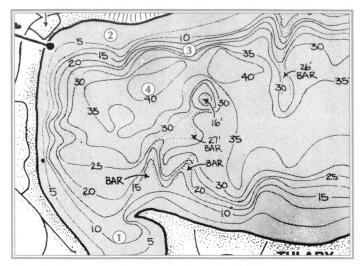

Good winter crappie spots include (1) shallow bays, (2) shallow weedy flats, (3) deep edges of flats and (4) deep holes.

From past experience, many anglers know the location of wintertime crappie holes on their favorite lakes. But if you have no idea where the crappies are, get a hydrographic map and look for the right kind of structure. Here's a common mistake made by many inexperienced crappie anglers: They presume crappies will be on the same type of structure as walleyes and other predator fish. You could say, in fact, that crappies prefer the opposite kind of structure that walleyes do. Instead of holding on humps, for instance, they're more likely to school up in holes or depressions. And instead of relating to points, they're more commonly found in sharp inside turns along a breakline.

If the ice is not too cloudy, good electronics will enable you to find the fish without drilling holes. Carry a spray bottle full of saltwater, squirt a little on the ice, hold your transducer in the puddle and take a reading. Crappies are easy to spot because of their habit of suspending well off the bottom. In a 40-foot hole, you might see the fish suspended at 25 or 30 feet. Keep moving and sounding until you find some fish, then drill several holes. I usually drill at least a dozen at a time. That way, if the fish move a little, I can stay with them.

By far the best bait I've found for this "run-and-shoot" offense is Normark's Jigging Rapala. I normally use a size 2 or 3 silver, although glow-in-the-dark colors, such as fire-tiger or glo-chartreuse, are good choices after sunset. The Jigging Rap has a lead body with a plastic tail fin that makes the bait dart to the side when you jig it. In 30 feet of water, the bait will dart sideways as much as 5 feet. Each time you jig, it darts out at a slightly different angle, so you'll eventually cover a 10-foot circle.

Here's the basic jigging strategy: Using a 24- to 30-inch medium-power graphite rod and a small spinning reel spooled with 6-pound mono, hold the bait just above the level of the fish and give it a sharp upward twitch. Then return the rod to the starting position and hold the tip still. You'll see the line move off to one side and then slowly settle back to the middle. Wait until the line stops moving before you jig again; practically all strikes come on the pause. Don't expect to feel a sharp jerk when a fish strikes; more often, you'll feel only a slight nudge, or the rod tip will come

HOW TO FISH A JIGGING RAP

Attach a Jigging Rap with a small clip. This reduces wear on your line and makes it easier to change baits.

Lower the bait until it's just a few inches above the fish, give it a sharp twitch and then return your rod to the original position.

up a bit. That means that a crappie has hit the bait from below. Set the hook immediately.

Jigging may not be the best strategy in very clear lakes. There, crappies can closely scrutinize your offering and they often turn up their noses at anything but real food. To make matters worse, they often feed only at night. The bite may not start until at least an hour after dark and it may last for only an hour or so. In this situation, it's tough to beat a 1½-inch fathead or shiner minnow fished on a size 4 hook beneath a small float. I prefer a sponge float for this kind of fishing. When the float ices up, just squeeze it and the ice crumbles away. H.T. Enterprises has improved on the traditional sponge float by adding a tiny cyalume light stick for night fishing.

If you're fishing in deep water, however, a fixed float can be a problem because it prevents you from reeling in your line. You have to haul the fish in hand over hand, so the line piles up and inevitably tangles or freezes to the ice or the floor of your fish shack, and you waste precious fishing time trying to get your bait back into the water.

Here's a better way, assuming the air temperature is above freezing or you're fishing inside a shelter. Fish the minnow on a slip-bobber rig, just as you would in summer. A slip-bobber knot on the line stops the bait when it reaches the desired depth, and the line slides through the bobber when you reel in a fish. This technique does not work well at below-freezing temperatures, because ice prevents the line from slipping through the bobber.

STERNBERG'S FAVORITE CRAPPIE BAITS & RIGS

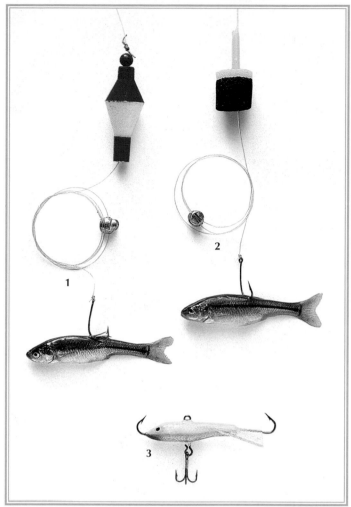

(1) Slip-bobber rig and minnow, for fishing inside a fish shack; (2) sponge float and minnow, for fishing outside (this model has a tiny cyalume light stick for night fishing); (3) size 3 Jigging Rapala, for covering water quickly.

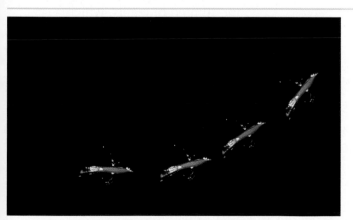

Pause while the lure darts out to the side and then returns to the center of the hole. While holding the rod still, wait for a tap or any upward movement of the rod tip, then set the hook.

Jig for several minutes in the same hole before moving on to the next hole. The lure will cover a large area around the hole in the pattern shown above.

A tear drop jig baited with a waxworm accounts for more winter 'gills than any other bait.

about the great bluegill fishing, chances are it's on the downhill slide," he warns. "You'd be much better off doing a little research and discovering a lake that's not as popular."

Here are Shodeen's recommendations for finding a "sleeper" lake for bull 'gills:

• Look for shallow, weedy lakes that periodically freeze out. Bluegills tend to overpopulate most lakes and become stunted. But in freeze-out lakes, an extremely heavy snow pack cuts off sunlight and prevents aquatic plants from producing oxygen through photosynthesis, killing most of the fish. A few live to reproduce the following spring, and with less food competition, the young grow rapidly. In three or four years, the lake is producing plate-size bluegills. Local fisheries managers can give you the names of known freeze-out lakes and tell you when they last froze out.

• Look for lakes that have been poisoned out, or "reclaimed," to improve the fish population. These lakes are commonly restocked with stunted bluegills netted from another nearby lake, resulting in an odd phenomenon. When the stunted bluegills, which are often several years old, are stocked into the void of a reclaimed lake, they grow at an astounding rate. It's as if they were compensating for the extremely slow growth in their early years of life. A bluegill that weighed only 3 ounces when stocked may grow to 12 or 14 ounces by the following year. This type of management greatly reduces the recovery time after reclamation and offers anglers a great opportunity to catch bull 'gills. Again, check with your local fisheries manager to get the names of lakes that have recently been reclaimed and stocked with bluegills.

Locational patterns for bluegills are similar to those mentioned earlier for crappies. You'll find them in shallow, weedy bays in early

Bluegills

A "bull 'gill" is one of ice fishing's top prizes. But these pug-nosed, hand-size members of the sunfish family are becoming harder and harder to find. "Once ice fishermen find a lake with big bluegills, they descend upon it in hordes," says Duane Shodeen, Metro Region Fisheries Supervisor for the Minnesota DNR. "I've seen anglers virtually wipe out a good bluegill lake in one winter season."

Shodeen, who is an avid winter bluegill angler, recommends staying away from lakes that are getting pounded. "Once you hear winter; but by midwinter most of the fish have moved into deep holes and inside turns on the breakline. And like crappies, bluegills will suspend over deep water, although the tendency is not quite as strong. When the spring thaw begins and meltwater starts to replenish oxygen levels, bluegills move back to the shallow bays.

Jigging is a recurring theme in modern ice fishing, and the story is no different for bluegills. Ultralight, ultra-sensitive graphite jigging rods and 2- to 4-pound monofilament line make it possible to detect even the lightest bluegill takes.

And just as electronics are indispensable in fishing for walleyes, lake trout and crappies, they're of utmost importance in bluegill fishing. Bluegills are not chasers; you often have to put the bait right in their faces and twitch it, jiggle it, lift it slowly or otherwise tease them into grabbing it. Make sure that the electronics you're using can pick up a tiny sunfish jig in water as deep as 30 feet. The Vexilar FL-8 and the Zercom LCF 40 are both sensitive enough to do the job.

Your choice of bluegill jigs depends on the water depth. Practically any jig will do in water less than 10 feet deep. But in deeper water, you'll need a fat-bodied jig that weighs at least 1/64 ounce, such as System Tackle's Fat Boy or H.T. Enterprises' Marmooska jig. Another good choice is the Fairy Jig, which has a pair of small flippers that create extra flash and attraction.

Thin, spoon-type jigs take too long to get down, and they aren't heavy enough to take all the kinks out of your line once they settle.

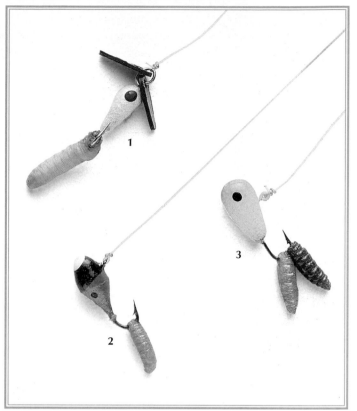

(1) Fairy Jig tipped with waxworm, (2) Marmooska Jig tipped with mousie, (3) Fat Boy tipped with Eurolarvae.

When a fish bites, you might not even notice, because the coiled line acts like a shock absorber. Tip the jig with some kind of insect larvae, such as a waxworm, spike, mousie, mealworm, goldenrod grub or Eurolarvae. Day in and day out, I've found that it's hard to beat a waxworm.

TIPS FOR ICING BULL 'GILLS

Ultralight, ultrasensitive graphite rods are ideal for jigging for bluegills. They respond to even the lightest take, making a spring-bobber unnecessary.

Hook a waxworm as shown, threading it on head first and then bringing the hook out about 1/4-inch down, so the bait hangs straight off the hook.

Don't jig with heavy mono and a light bait. The bait is not heavy enough to remove the kinks from the line, so the feel of a take may be absorbed.

Yellow Perch

Finding yellow perch is not a challenge. Small to medium-size perch abound in practically any lake that has walleyes. But finding "jumbo" perch is another matter. Surprisingly few lakes hold good populations of perch weighing 12 ounces or more, and when it comes to super-jumbos (those weighing 24 ounces or more), you can count the lakes on the fingers of both hands.

Large midwestern walleye waters are the best bet for a pail-full of jumbos. Good choices include Mille Lacs, Leech and Winnibigoshish in Minnesota, Spirit Lake in Iowa and Saginaw Bay of Lake Huron. Some perch addicts regard Ontario's Lake Simcoe as the best perch lake of all. If you're into the super-jumbos, look toward the alkali lakes of the Dakotas. These waters teem with freshwater shrimp, a tiny crustacean that makes perch grow to outlandish sizes. South Dakota's top pick is Lake Poinsett; North Dakota's is Devil's Lake, which once produced a 2-pound, 15½ ouncer, the current state record.

You'll find perch on the same kind of structure that holds walleyes, and often you'll catch both species out of the same hole. But perch have a habit of moving away from the structure and holding over a flat, muddy bottom, especially in midday. If you're not finding fish right on the structure, use your electronics and you may find them as much as 200 yards off the structure.

Small perch bite anytime, but jumbos are notoriously fussy. They may feed for only an hour or so each day, and you don't necessarily know when that hour will be. Sometimes they're into the dusk and dawn feeding pattern; other times, it's a noon to 2 bite. Oddly enough, I've never seen too much correlation with the weather. In most lakes, perch bite well in early winter and even better in late winter, when the ice starts to honeycomb.

When the bite is on, you'll catch fish as fast as you can get your line up and down the hole, and it doesn't much matter what you're using for bait. When it's not, you can still catch a few fish, but you'll have to "finesse" them.

I normally jig for perch using the same outfit I use for walleyes – a sensitive 30-inch graphite rod (medium power) and a small spinning reel spooled with 6-pound mono. I also use a lot of the same jigging baits – like a size 3 Swedish Pimple tipped with a minnow head or perch eye, and a size 3 Jigging Rapala. When it's necessary to finesse them, I prefer a dropper rig. To make this rig, take the smallest size Kastmaster or Do-Jigger spoon, remove the hook, and replace it with a size 6 single hook on a 4-inch, 6-pound-test mono dropper. Bait the hook with two or three waxworms or a perch eye, lower it to within 6 inches of the bottom, lift it a foot or so, and let it flutter back down. Then just hold it steady for several seconds. That's usually when the perch bite.

Whatever bait you use, be sure to periodically drop it to the bottom, because perch are known for their habit of slurping insect larvae right out of the bottom mud. When you lift the bait, there might be a jumbo perch hanging on it.

Here are a few tricks that will boost your odds when perch fishing gets tough:

•Try dead-stickin'. Make a small pile of slush-ice just in front of your fishing hole and set your rod on the pile so at least a foot of the rodtip extends over the hole. Or, set your rod in a rod holder that fits on the lip of your bucket. Adjust the depth so the hook of your dropper rig is just above the bottom, then sit back and watch the rod tip. If it wiggles even the slightest bit, set the hook.

•Tease the fish up. With good electronics, you'll be able to see perch looking at your bait. If you jig it at their level, they'll follow it for awhile, but will eventually lose interest and disappear. Instead, bring the bait up slow-

STERNBERG'S FAVORITE PERCH BAITS

(1) Size 3 Swedish Pimple tipped with minnow head, (2) Do-Jigger Spoon with 4-inch dropper and size 6 hook baited with waxworms, (3) size 3 Jigging Rapala, (4) mayfly wiggler on size 10 Aberdeen hook.

ly, stopping to jig it a little along the way. I've had perch follow the bait up as much as 20 feet before grabbing it. Evidently, they make a last-minute decision to take it before it gets away.

•When all else fails, try a mayfly wiggler. If there ever was a magic perch bait, this is it. The problem with wigglers is keeping them on the hook. They're very delicate and a nibbling perch can easily strip them off without you knowing it. Try threading them head-first onto a size 10 long-shank Aberdeen hook on a dropper rig. Again, set the hook at the least indication of a bite.

Used to be, catching panfish through the ice was no big deal. They were super-abundant, and on a given day most anybody with a little ice-fishing savvy could easily fill most of a 5-gallon pail. That's not the case today. Finding good-sized panfish is a challenge, and so is catching them. On heavily pressured lakes, they've seen every bait imaginable, so you'll have to dig deep into your bag of tricks. And if you're lucky enough to discover a lake with a good crop of uneducated, braggin'-sized panfish, don't tell a soul.

ON THE TRAIL OF BULL 'GILLS

By Jack Gulnetti

With the recent explosion of interest in tournament fishing, there is a glut of information on techniques and equipment used for the most popular tournament species – bass, walleyes and salmon.

But what about panfish? Where can we find expert advice on what may well be the nation's favorite fish, the bluegill? More angling hours are devoted to this species than any other, but there is a definite shortage of reliable, scientific information, particularly on the specifics of finding and catching bull 'gills – those pug-nosed, plate-sized fighters that you can't quite wrap your hand around.

This fact is precisely what led Jeff Murray, a well-known outdoor writer from northern Minnesota, on a relentless pursuit of solid information about trophy bluegills. What Murray has learned might surprise you. It may also help you locate and catch the biggest bluegills your area has to offer.

"What started it all," Murray recalled, "was the day I latched onto my first true bull 'gill – a 1 1/2 pounder. It happened while I was back-trolling for walleyes. I mean, the fish looked like some sort of mutant, but in a striking sort of way. From that moment, I was hooked!"

But Murray soon found out that the trail to bluegill heaven was littered with road-blocks. The biggest was the deficiency of information in fishing literature on the habits of bull 'gills.

"I quickly realized that very few anglers – or biologists – knew much about large bluegills," Murray said. "They were like me – the ones they caught were accidents, and the others taken on purpose were, well, embellished somewhat. Everybody, it seems, thinks 1/2-pounders are 1-pounders. Few have come face to face with a true bull 'gill!"

This left Murray with only one option: Search scientific journals, doctorate theses, test-net surveys and fisheries reports. This approach eventually paid off. He soon began to find information that would lead him to trophy bluegills.

The major requirement for big bluegills, Murray discovered, is enough predators to keep the number of smaller 'gills in check. "Because bluegills are such prolific spawners, something has to offset their ability to overrun the food supply," Murray says. "As a rule, I avoid lakes with a lot of runts. They're a red flag that stunting has occurred. You're just wasting your time!"

A good population of bass or other predators is necessary to control the bluegill population. Look at the numbers of bluegill fry in this photo.

Lakes with this much spawning habitat are not likely to produce bull 'gills.

According to a 56-page pamphlet, *Producing Fish And Wildlife From Kansas Ponds,* farm pond fishermen who wish to grow huge bluegills can do so. It's easy: Stock bass with the 'gills and release every bass you catch under 15 inches. This keeps the predator-prey ratio in balance.

In many northern lakes, yellow perch help keep bluegill numbers in check. Research conducted by Dennis Anderson, a Minnesota DNR fisheries biologist, found this relationship in natural lakes of more than 300 acres with sparse vegetation. "I never appreciated the role perch play until I caught a handful of them last winter on a favorite bluegill lake," Murray recalls. "Each one was regurgitating 1/2-inch 'gills on the way up the ice hole. Perch are more predacious than I'd given them credit for!"

Another important requirement is an environment favorable to efficient predation on young bluegills. The water must be clear enough to allow bluegills to feed on tiny crustaceans and enable predators, such as bass, perch and northern pike, to prey on small 'gills.

Spawning habitat should also be restricted. Because bluegills guard their spawning beds,

a high percentage of their young survive. Sand or gravel shorelines make ideal bluegill spawning habitat, but if there is too much of this type of bottom, nesting is *too* successful. There should be a fair amount of muck and rock to balance things out.

Lakes that undergo a periodic drawdown are often good choices for bull 'gills. In flowage lakes where utility companies control riparian rights, for instance, water levels fluctuate on a seasonal basis. "During low-water conditions, young bluegills are forced out of shoreline vegetation and into open water, where they're exposed to predators ," Murray explains. "That keeps their population in check."

Even if you're lucky enough to discover a lake with big 'gills, you still have to locate them, and that is often the rub. But a study conducted on Michigan's Third Sister Lake offers some locational clues. The study showed that bluegills have a sedentary nature; if the habitat meet its basic needs, a bluegill doesn't move far over the course of the year. Of 27 bluegills tagged in the study, 18 of them moved no more than 65 yards from the point of original capture. So once you find a good bluegill spot, the fish probably won't be far from there next time you come back.

Murray's Bluegill Condo

Murray has fished bluegills in a variety of waters and carefully noted what components are needed to make a prime bluegill spot. "If I had to design a bluegill 'condo,' here's what it would look like:"

"It would be a large bay off the main lake with easy access to deep water. The bay would have good structure, like a weedy hump, to hold fish in summer, and a small, shallow connecting bay with a sandy bottom and plenty of woody cover for spawning habitat. Preferably, the bay would have a southern exposure, so it would start to warm early in spring.

"I know of several bluegill spots that meet those specifications," Murray says, "and they commonly produce bluegills pushing a pound."

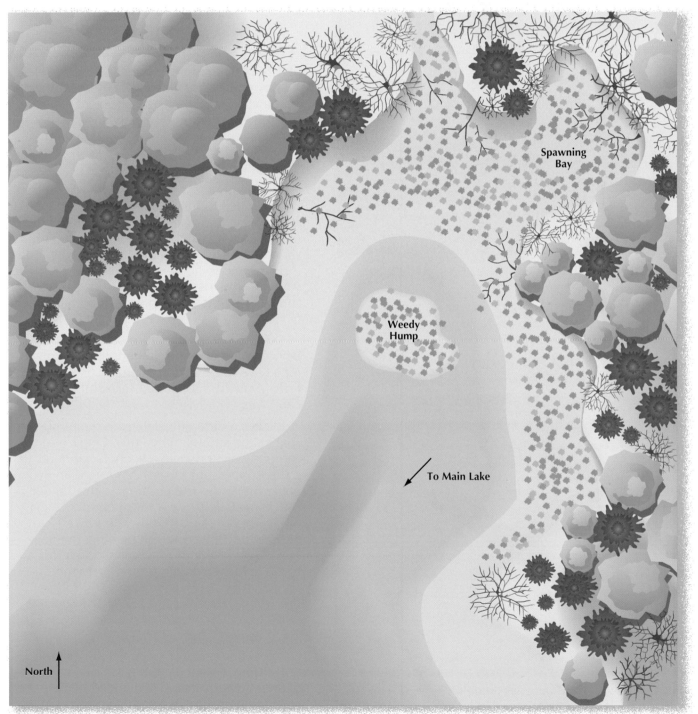

A large bay with all the elements of a "bluegill condo."

Baits, Lures & Techniques for Bull 'Gills

A 'gill like this is a prize in any body of water.

MURRAY'S FAVORITE BLUEGILL BAITS

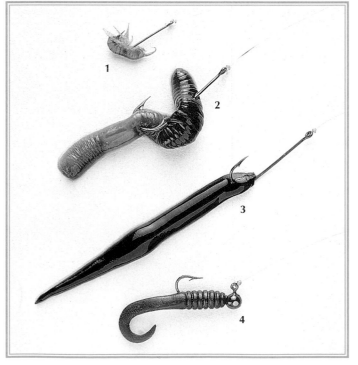

(1) Gammarus (also known as "shrimp" or "scud") on size 10 hook, (2) half crawler on size 6 hook, (3) small leech on size 8 hook, (4) 1/64-ounce curlytail jig.

"The best time to catch trophy 'gills is when they're concentrated in their spawning areas," Murray contends. "Bluegills of all sizes attempt to spawn, but the biggest fish select the superior spawning sites. Invariably, they'll be just deep enough so you won't see them and they'll build their nests in areas with plenty of logs, fallen trees and brush."

Murray prefers a neutrally-buoyant presentation to tempt finicky spawners. "Start with a featherweight rod – a fly rod blank about 8 feet long, tied with single-foot spinning guides. It shouldn't weigh much over two ounces. Add 2-pound mono and a small spinning reel. This way, you can toss a variety of baits – freshwater shrimp, small leeches, pieces of nightcrawler or maggots – with no extra weight."

"Keep a low profile, turn off the motor well before you reach your intended target, make long casts to avoid spooking the fish and pull them away from their beds as soon as you can," Murray advises.

It takes a different strategy to tempt post-spawn and summertime 'gills. One simple technique is to dangle a lively leech beneath a slip bobber, but Murray has found an even better method. "The problem with summer fish, especially those over a pound, is their on-again, off-again moods," he says. "One minute they'll hit a radish peeling, the next they'll ignore the most tantalizing offering. If you're lucky enough to find them in a cooperative mood, use whatever you want. But when they're fussy, I like to use shrimp."

When Murray uses the term "shrimp," he's referring to 1/4- to 1/2-inch long crustaceans called Gammarus, which are technically scuds, not shrimp. "Most big bluegill waters are full of them," Murray says. "They're definitely the ticket when fishing is tough, although you'll have to sort through more smaller fish.

"If your bait shop doesn't carry shrimp (scuds), you can mimic them with a 1/64-ounce jig and a soft-plastic grub body. Cast it out using light line and a long rod and let it settle into the strike zone. Then, work the jig back in short, quick, two-inch strokes."

"This presentation accomplishes two things. First, it imitates the way shrimp propel themselves through the water. Second, the light line and long rod help register a bite before the fish has a chance to spit the jig."

There's a lot more to bluegill fishing than soaking a worm below a bobber. But the best technique in the world won't produce big 'gills if you're not on the right water. Murray's tips will boost your odds of finding 'gills that won't fit in your frying pan.

HOW TO CATCH BULL 'GILLS

Push a "shrimp" (also known as "scud") onto a fine-wire, size 10 hook as shown. The natural curl of the bait should match the bend of the hook.

Use a long rod and light line to cast the unweighted bait or to drop the bait into a hard-to-reach pocket in the cover.

Stay low and make extra-long casts to prevent the fish from seeing you.

Set the hook immediately when you feel a bite and try to pull the fish away from the spawning area so it doesn't spook other fish.

Walleye

Tournament pros have proven that there's a lot more to walleye fishing than dragging bait on the bottom.

BIG-RIVER WALLEYES

by Chris Niskanen

Dave Lincoln's life, in many ways, has aways been connected to river walleye fishing. One of the Midwest's finest walleye rivers – the Mississippi – makes a graceful turn along the eastern boundary of Lincoln's hometown of Dubuque, Iowa. And for 17 years, Lincoln was co-owner of a sporting goods department at a local hardware store, selling fishing tackle to area walleye gurus and learning their secrets.

Lincoln, who now runs his own tackle store, started out as a bass fisherman. "I fished

bass tournaments for 10 years," he said, "but I also really loved jigging for walleyes."

When Lincoln got serious about river-walleye fishing, he teamed up with one of those local walleye gurus, Art Lehrman, to hit the Masters Walleye Circuit. The newcomers soon established themselves as one of the premier teams on the tourney trail, winning the MWC's World Championship in 1990.

The pair's success came by finding walleyes in places that other anglers overlooked. Their habit of staying away from the crowds has made Lincoln and Lehrman somewhat of an mystery on the Masters Walleye Circuit.

Walleyes are a river's nomads, migrating on a seasonal basis to find habitat conducive to feeding and spawning. So when tournament anglers find the walleyes, it's not

Riprap banks have many crevices that hold aquatic insects, which in turn draw baitfish. The baitfish draw walleyes.

Wing dams are man-made current deflectors made of rocks and logs that channel the flow toward the center of the river.

uncommon for 30 or more boats to be fishing one area. But you won't find Lincoln or Lehrman among them.

The team fishes the type of riprap and wing-dam structure that is well-known to river walleye anglers. But they also have discovered something that the Corps of Engineers calls "submerged bank protection," a type of structure that is new territory to most walleye fishermen.

In spring, they often focus on creek mouths. Frequently, the creeks are a little warmer than the main river, so they draw baitfish. While river walleyes do not travel far up creeks, they often congregate near the mouths to feed. Inflowing creeks also create eddies that enable walleyes to escape the current.

The secret to successful river fishing is knowing when and how to fish each of these habitats.

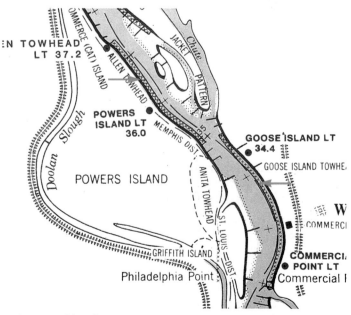

Submerged bank protection (green arrows on the chart above) is a form of underwater riprap that prevents bank erosion. River charts like this help you find this habitat.

Casting small plastic-bodied jigs to riprap banks is a dynamite technique for big early-spring walleyes.

Jig Fishing
Techniques for Big Rivers

In spring, Lincoln and Lehrman hit the river as soon as there is open water – even if it means bumping a few floating ice chunks. Spring walleyes are searching for spawning areas, and one of the most popular spots to fish are tailwaters below dams.

While many fishermen dodge each other in the dam tailwaters, these anglers cast small jigs along downstream riprap shorelines, where walleyes also spawn.

"We don't even go close to tailwaters anymore because everyone else is there," Lincoln says. "You can also get bigger fish downstream. Riprap is one of our favorite spots. We'll be fishing very shallow, from 6 to 8 feet."

The pair doesn't anchor but moves constantly, casting jigs tipped with plastic tails or minnows. Or, they may vertically jig while using their bow-mount trolling motor to keep the

boat drifting at exactly the same speed as the current. They normally use 1/8- to 3/8-ounce jigs tipped with minnows.

Stinger hooks are a must when tipping with minnows for light-biting spring walleyes. Instead of bringing back a minnow with a chewed-up tail, you'll hook the fish in the lip.

"There aren't many guys who fish an eight-hour tournament using only plastics," Lehman notes. "But we often do. Plastics work year-round. Art usually starts by using plastics and I may start with live bait, but the plastics normally work better, except when the fish are sluggish in winter."

To die-hard river anglers who rarely use anything but a jig-and-minnow combination, that statement may seem hard to believe. But this duo has spent thousands of hours perfecting the right presentations using jigs and plastics. Their favorite is a jig with a plastic shad body, a combination that Lincoln calls "matching the hatch."

"There are a zillion shad in the river," Lincoln says. "Fish see the body shape and the shine of the plastic shad body, and that's what they snap at."

"We once ran the boat all the way up to Guttenberg, Iowa, and hit almost all the wing dams along the way. We caught walleyes on practically every one using shad bodies. It was crazy. Sometimes we even had doubles on."

Lincoln recommends using 2½-inch shad bodies for ⅛- and ¼-ounce jigs; 3-inchers for larger jigs. Their favorite color is pearl blue with a black stripe on the back.

When they are not using shad bodies, the pair opts for curlytails in motor oil, chartreuse and fire cracker colors.

They prefer jig heads in two-tone chartreuse and orange, blue, plain orange, plain chartreuse and pink.

Whether they're fishing shad bodies or curlytails, Lincoln believes lighter jigs are best. Inexperienced river walleye anglers always use a heavy jig to keep in constant touch with the bottom – no matter how strong the current.

"On about every third bounce, you'll get snagged," Lincoln says. "You want to go as light as you can and still stay in the fish zone." A lighter jig sinks more slowly, too, giving the fish more time to grab it.

"Of course, you can't use light jigs in strong current. On some wing dams, you'll get blown away with an eighth-ounce jig. But you should be able to get down with a quarter ounce."

For fishing lightweight jigs (⅛- to ¼-ounce), Lincoln recommends a 6-foot, medium-power, fast-action spinning outfit spooled with 6- to 8-pound test mono.

LINCOLN & LEHRMAN'S FAVORITE JIGS

(1) Fireball jig and stinger tipped with minnow, (2) & (3) Sassy Shad, (4) & (5) Berkley Power Grub, (6) Gator tail Grub (firecracker).

JIG FISHING TIPS

Keep your line as close to vertical as possible when vertically jigging. If you let your line drag at too much of an angle, you won't feel subtle takes.

Keep your rod tip low when jigging in the wind. Otherwise, the wind will catch your line, forming a large bow and making it difficult to feel your strikes.

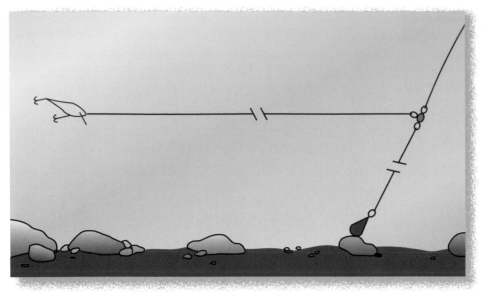

Three-way rigs enable you to keep your bait or lure close to the bottom without constantly hanging up. The weight occasionally bounces bottom, but the lure runs about a foot above it.

How to Fish Three-Way Rigs

As the water warms in summer, walleyes migrate to wing dams and other rocky areas near the main channel. The duo usually fishes the upstream face of a wing dam using a 3-way rig.

"Trolling a 3-way rig with live bait across the face of a wing dam isn't as easy as it sounds," Lincoln warns. He said it was the most difficult technique he had to master.

"Art used to take me out to fish three-ways, and he'd always make sure I caught fish," Lincoln recalls. "It took me about half a season to learn it. The trick is telling the difference between a walleye strike and the rig bouncing along the rocks. A walleye doesn't always hit a live-bait rig as hard as a crankbait. Of course, it's something that can't be learned by reading, it just takes practice."

Precise boat control is a must in working wing dams. You not only have to know how to maneuver the boat, you must become familiar with the specific wing dam you're fishing. Every wing dam is different, with a different current flow and configuration. You need to know how big it is, where the current speed is right and where there are crevices, nooks or exposed rocks.

For fishing three-way rigs, Lincoln uses a medium-action baitcasting outfit with 10-pound mono.

Other prime summertime spots are areas with submerged bank protection. This rocky structure is essentially underwater riprap, placed along river bends and straight shorelines by the U.S. Army Corps of Engineers to prevent erosion. Because it's submerged, you may have to use electronics to find it. Submerged bank protection holds fish well into the fall.

Once you find it, you can use a variety of lures to fish it. "We'll troll three-way rigs along it, jig it, or cast to it with crankbaits," Lincoln says.

Obtaining a good river map, such as the Mississippi River navigation charts published by the U.S. Army Corps of Engineers, is a big help in locating submerged bank protection. The problem is, it is not always along the bank. A river is constantly changing course and, in many places, will wash out a channel behind the bank protection, so the rocks are now located well off shore.

Besides perfecting all the techniques for fishing different kinds of river habitat, river anglers also have to contend with a variable that has little effect on lake fishing – fluctuating water levels.

This fluctuation can play havoc on walleyes and an angler's ability to catch them. "A lot depends on how drastically the river has changed," Lincoln says. "I'd rather not fish a river that is dropping; I'd just as soon have it coming up a bit. It doesn't seem to bother the fish as much. But either way, it's not worth a darn if it's a drastic change. If the river is coming up, we'll fish shallow. If it's dropping, we fish a little deeper."

Although river walleye fishing can be a challenge, anglers like Lincoln and Lehrman have been instrumental in breaking the "copycat syndrome" that had become so prevalent among river fishermen. But don't expect them to reveal their secret spots; you'll have to pay your dues to find the fish – just like they did.

Rigs for River Fishing

Lincoln and Lehrman prefer 3-way swivel rigs to fish live bait, crankbaits and minnowbaits. A 3-way rig consists of the swivel, a 12- to 15-inch dropline attached to a weight and a 3-to 4-foot leader.

With crankbaits and minnowbaits, the rig is usually weighted with a 1- to 2-ounce bell sinker. With live bait, which is fished much more slowly, the weight is a ⅜- to ⅝-ounce jig tipped with a plastic shad body. The jig not only makes a good weight, sometimes walleyes grab it instead of the live bait.

"We'll use minnowbaits on wing dams as early as possible in the summer," Lincoln says. They prefer Bomber Long A or a floating Rapala, in either orange or chartreuse. Crayfish-colored crankbaits work well in late summer.

"If you want to use live bait, nothing can beat the old nightcrawler for walleye fishing," Lincoln claims. "But leeches work well too." The bait is usually fished on a plain, No. 4 Tru-turn hook or a floating jig head. Often, the anglers use beads or spinners ahead of a nightcrawler for extra attraction.

Three-way rig with a size 6 hook baited with a nightcrawler and a ½-ounce jig for weight.

Three-way rig with minnowbait or crankbaits and a 1-ounce bell sinker.

HOW TO FISH A WING DAM

Walleyes usually hold along the upstream face of a wing dam, which is the prime feeding location. They can rest in the eddy that forms above the wing dam (inset) and pick off food carried to them by the current. Lincoln and Lehrman prefer to troll across the upstream face of a wing dam using 3-way rigs, but many anglers opt to anchor above a wing dam, pitch plastic-bodied jigs onto the top of the dam and then retrieve them down the upstream face.

EARLY-SEASON WALLEYES

by Dick Sternberg

Long before the snow has disappeared, anglers across the Northcountry start showing the symptoms of walleye fever. They religiously watch the TV fishing shows, buy the new fishing videos and intently study fishing magazines, hoping to unearth a nugget of walleye-fishing information that will tip the odds in their favor once the season begins.

But whenever I hear about the latest walleye-fishing "breakthrough," I can't help but wonder why the best walleye anglers I know seem to do things pretty much like they always have. Rather than spending their time messing with new techniques or new equipment, they concentrate on finding aggressive fish, then use time-proven methods to catch them.

Practically all the top walleye anglers throw a jig and minnow in early season, or they might switch to a minnowbait if the fish are really turned on. Finding the active fish is way more important than what you throw at them.

The key word is ACTIVE, meaning that the fish are moving around and feeding. Even under the best of conditions, walleyes tend to be finicky biters. But in early season, when the water is cold and they're still recuperating from the rigors of spawning, getting them to open their mouths may be next to impossible.

My best advice when walleyes are in this kind of mood: go someplace where they're not. If it's a late spring and the water is too cold, that someplace may be a shallower lake, a lake farther south or maybe a river where the walleyes spawned earlier. On the other hand, if spring comes early, the walleye bite in these waters may be winding down, and you'd do better on a deeper lake or one farther north.

To determine whether a given lake is likely to produce in early season, ask the following questions of a knowledgeable local source, such as a bait-shop operator, fisheries manager or NAFC Fishing Information Network (F.I.N.) Affiliate:

- When did the ice go out? As a rule, the walleye bite won't get into full-swing until at least a month after ice-out. If the weather after ice-out is unseasonably cold, it may take a week or two longer for the fish to come around.

- When did the walleyes finish spawning? This question has little relevance if you're not concerned with size, but if you're interested in big fish, it's of utmost importance. Female walleyes – the biggest ones – feed very little once spawning begins and generally refuse to bite during the two weeks following spawning. Then, feeding activity gradually picks up, but it doesn't peak until much later than most anglers think. The very best big-fish action generally begins about six weeks after spawning and lasts for about 10 days.

- What is the water temperature? Walleyes generally spawn in the upper 40s, so temperatures in that range or below may indicate that they have not completed spawning or are still in the post-spawn recuperation phase.

If you don't get the right answers to these questions, you may want to revise your fishing plans.

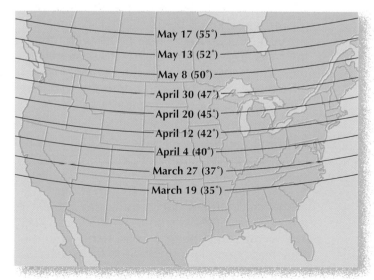

At a latitude of 50° N., walleye spawning activity peaks on May 8 in an average year. At a latitude of 40°, it peaks on April 4, more than a month earlier. But the peak could be as much as 10 days earlier or later, depending on the weather.

Big walleye lakes like Minnesota's Mille Lacs draw huge crowds on opening day. Fishermen flock to these lakes because of tradition, even though the conditions in a particular year may be a lot better on a smaller, lesser-known lake.

Hang Loose for Early Season 'Eyes

One of the main reasons anglers fail to catch walleyes on the opener is that they're too strongly bound by tradition. Opening day means going up to the lake cabin with the family or to a favorite resort with some buddies. They never even consider going anywhere else. But when you commit yourself to fishing a certain body of water, your options for finding active fish are limited.

Even though I know better, the Minnesota custom of going "up north" for the walleye opener sometimes overrides common sense. A few years ago, I decided to join some friends for their annual opening-day extravaganza on Minnesota's famed Mille Lacs Lake. The weather had been unseasonably cold, but they had been planning the trip for weeks, and I didn't want to cancel out on them. When we hit the water on opening-day morning, my surface temperature gauge registered 38° F, so I had a pretty good idea of what was in store for us. In a day and a half, we caught

a total of 8 small walleyes – all males that were still dripping milt.

By noon of the second day, I'd seen enough, so I headed home. I live near a lake in the western suburbs of Minneapolis, and I decided to give it a try before calling it a weekend. In less than two hours, I caught 16 nice walleyes within a few minutes of the boat landing. Moving 100 miles south made all the difference.

The lesson is to "hang loose," keeping your options open as long as possible. This way, you can see how the season is progressing and then plan your strategy accordingly. Even if you can't go far, don't be afraid to try other nearby lakes if you find that conditions aren't right on yours. I've seen times when the walleyes were completely turned off in a deep, clear lake, but biting like crazy in a shallow, dark-water lake only a few miles away.

Many anglers hesitate to try different waters because they're not confident of their abilities to locate fish. It's a lot easier to go to a familiar spot on a familiar lake. But armed with modern electronics and a good understanding of the effects of wind, finding walleyes on a strange lake can be a lot easier than you think.

Electronics –
Key to Finding Early
Season Walleyes

For scouting new water, I prefer a video sonar with a fast chart speed, such as the Si-Tex CVS 106. The fast chart speed is critical. It enables you to graph fish while traveling at speeds of 20 mph or more, so you can cover water – and find fish – in a hurry. If you moved that fast with a slow-speed graph, the fish marks would be so narrow you wouldn't even notice them. Most liquid-crystal graphs are not fast enough for high-speed sounding.

In order to get a good high-speed signal, your transducer must be properly adjusted. The face of the transducer should be about 1/4 inch below the bottom of the boat and tilted back about 5 degrees. If the face is level or tilted forward, the transducer will create so much turbulence that you won't get a decent high-speed reading. If the boat bottom has ribs, position the transducer midway between a pair of them.

Here's another early-season graphing tip. Use a transducer with a narrow cone angle to minimize your "dead zone" (diagram below). When the water is cold, walleyes may be difficult to graph because they often lie very close to the bottom. With a wide cone, you simply won't see many of these fish. When the water warms and walleyes get more active, you should have no trouble graphing them with a wide cone.

In early season, you're more likely to find walleyes along shoreline breaks than on mid-lake structure. All you have to do is closely watch the graph while following the breakline. Veer in and out as you motor along, varying your depth until you see some fish. Chances are, you'll find them at depths of 20 feet or less, usually on gradually sloping points or other irregularities along the breakline. A sensitive graph will also show you differences in bottom hardness. A firm bottom shows as a solid band with a sharp, distinct top edge; a soft bottom has a fuzzy top edge. Walleyes will nearly always hold over a firm bottom.

Once you spot fish, stop immediately and fish your way back through them. Continue this process until you find a school of walleyes that are feeding. Using this technique, it's possible to scout most of the likely structure in a small lake in only an hour or two.

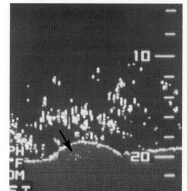

Look for humps on the bottom with "air" beneath them. The air is a telltale sign that the humps are really fish. If they were rocks, you would not see the air (arrow).

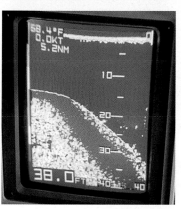

Find hard bottom by looking for a thick band with a sharp upper edge (left side of screen). A soft bottom has a fuzzy upper edge.

Every depth finder has "blind spots" (red zone), the size of which depend on the cone angle of the transducer and the water depth. This explains why a narrow cone is best for early season fishing, when walleyes are hugging bottom.

Successful early-season walleye anglers work windy shorelines and points, rather than lee shores.

Playing the Wind for Early-Season Walleyes

You can improve your odds of finding active fish by paying close attention to the wind. Although wind is important any time of year, it has even more significance in spring. After a day or two of warm weather, for instance, the surface temperature increases by several degrees. Then, a moderate to strong wind will push the warm surface layer to the windward shore.

Not only does the warmer water stimulate the walleyes to feed, the wind stirs up bottom materials, darkening the water and creating the low-light environment in which walleyes feel comfortable. Walleyes begin moving to the windward shore shortly after the wind starts to blow. The longer it continues to blow from the same direction, the greater the number of fish that will move in.

Ironically, most anglers head for the lee side of the lake in windy weather. There, they won't have to worry about getting splashed by waves – and they also won't be bothered by walleyes biting on their line. Not only is the water much colder, it's also much clearer – not the combination you want for a good walleye bite.

One of the most productive spots along a windward shore is a distinct bay, because it collects the warm water and prevents it from mixing with adjacent cold water, as it would along a straight shoreline. An equally good spot, but one that's harder to recognize, is a sharp indentation in the breakline – sort of an underwater bay. Let's say there's a 5-foot-deep flat running a block out from shore and then dropping quickly into deep water. But on that flat is a 15-foot deep trough that starts at the outer drop and extends almost all the way to shore. That trough will trap any warm water that blows into it. There may be no visual clue that such spots even exist, but you can find them by checking a hydrographic map. I've seen water temperatures in these bays and breakline troughs as much as 10 degrees warmer than on the lee shore, so it's no wonder they're walleye magnets.

While scouting a new lake on the Wisconsin opener several years back, I stumbled onto a trough like the one I described. I was fishing with a friend who had caught only a handful of walleyes in his whole life, so I was astounded when he pitched out his jig, reeled it a few feet and hooked a nice walleye. And I was even more astounded when he did it again a couple minutes later. I wasn't getting any hits, so I watched closely to see what he was doing. Instead of bumping the jig slowly along bottom, as you'd normally do in early season, he was reeling it like a crankbait. When he hooked a fair-sized muskie and then a big smallmouth bass, I decided it was time to switch tactics. The fish were so aggressive, they were swimming high off the bottom, probably chasing minnows drawn in by the warm water, and the fast crankbait retrieve was exactly what they wanted.

That's an example of what can happen when you find active fish. It also explains why the most knowledgeable walleye anglers spend their time looking for biters, rather than trying to trigger non-biters. Why not give these locational strategies a try – they'll put more walleyes in your boat than all the latest gadgets and hottest new baits possibly could.

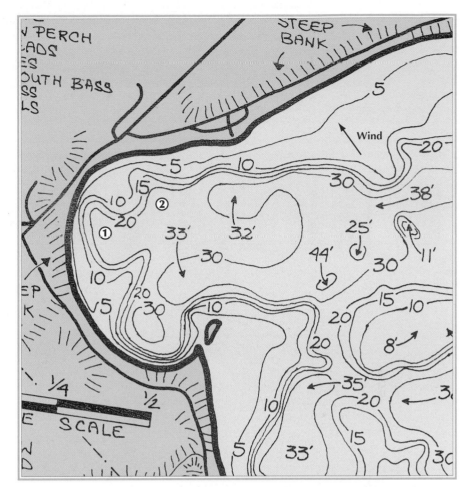

Indentations in breaklines along the downwind shore (1 and 2) are ideal spots for early spring walleyes. The warm water blown in by the wind collects in these pockets, making them several degrees warmer than the surrounding water. An accurate lake map will help you pinpoint the most likely pockets.

Look for mudlines that form along a windward shore. The wind stirs up the bottom and blows in warm water, which draws baitfish and, in turn, walleyes. Because of the reduced clarity, walleyes are not hesitant to feed.

JIGGING FOR HARDWATER WALLEYES

by Dick Sternberg

Walleye fishing is tough enough during the open-water season, when you're able to move about and explore the structure with your electronics. When ice cover prevents you from doing that exploring, you face an even greater challenge.

As in most other kinds of ice fishing, the key to catching walleyes is mobility. You can't wait for the fish to come to you; you have to go to them. That means cutting a lot of holes and staying on the move.

Sure, the guy who waits them out by still-fishing with a minnow beneath a float, rattle reel or tip-up will occasionally score big, but the guy who keeps moving will have more consistent success.

Not too many years back, live minnows accounted for practically all wintertime walleyes. Now, the best ice anglers rarely use them. They rely almost exclusively on jigging baits, sometimes tipping them with minnow heads or perch eyes for a little extra attraction.

Until a few years ago, I'd hang a live minnow from a tip-up, and jig with another line. But on most days, I'd catch a dozen walleyes

jigging for every one I caught on the minnow. Now, I rarely put out a minnow because it's just not worth the extra hassle.

The problem is, every time you move a minnow line, you have to reset the depth to keep the bait just inches off bottom. And some states have laws that require you stay within so many feet of your line, so if you're using a stationary line, your mobility is greatly restricted. When you're jigging, you don't have to worry about setting the depth, so it's no trouble at all to move to another hole.

You can catch walleyes on a wide variety of jigging baits, including spoons like the Vingla and Swedish Pimple, swimming baits like the Jigging Rapala, and vibrating blades like the Cicada and Heddon Sonar. You can also use a plain leadhead jig, tipped with a minnow or minnow head. My favorite is a size 4 Swedish Pimple (silver with a green or chartreuse back) tipped with a minnow head. If you use the entire minnow, you'll get too many short strikes.

Using a 30-inch graphite rod and a small spinning reel spooled with 6-pound mono, simply lower the spoon to the bottom, reel it

POPULAR JIGGING BAITS

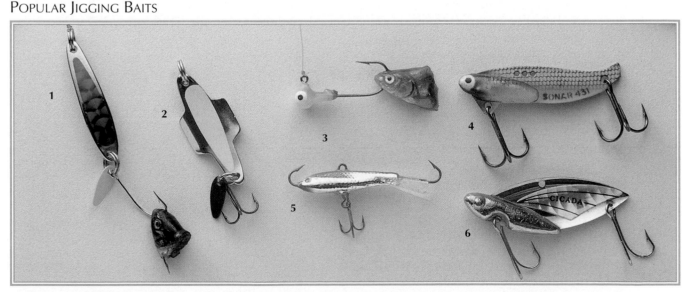

(1) Size 4 Swedish Pimple tipped with minnow head, (2) size 4 Vingla, (3) ⅛-ounce jig and minnow head, (4) ¼-ounce Heddon Sonar, (5) size 5 Jigging Rapala, (6) ⅛-ounce Cicada.

Hook keeper

Genuine cork handle

Small open-face spinning reel with smooth drag

up 6 to 12 inches and then give it a gentle twitch. Hold the rodtip stationary as the spoon sinks; it will flutter out to the side before settling to rest in the original position. Don't jig again until the spoon has completely stopped moving. Most strikes come after all movement has stopped.

A sensitive flasher, such as a Zercom LCF-40 or a Vexilar FL-8, is a big help for this type of fishing. The Zercom has more power, but the Vexilar has a color display. A walleye hanging a few feet off to the side of the bait shows up as a green band or a thin, red one. But as the fish moves nearer to the bait, the green band turns red or the width of the red band increases. With a little experience, you'll know exactly what's going on beneath you.

If you jig in a hole for five minutes or so and don't see a fish or get a strike, reel up and move to another hole. Experiment with the intensity of your twitches and the length of the pause between twitches to determine the action the walleyes prefer on a given day. Watch the flasher closely to see how the fish are responding and adjust your action accordingly. Sometimes the best action is to prop your rod up on a clump of snow and don't jig it at all. Watch the rodtip for even the slightest movement; if you see anything, set the hook immediately.

To maximize your odds with this jigging system, you'll need to find some good walleye structure like a sunken island, a sharp point or inside turn on a breakline. If you own a handheld GPS, you can save a lot of scouting time by punching in one of your summertime walleye holes. After finding the structure, drill a series of holes along the break. You could drill a hole first, check its depth and then move as necessary until you find the desired depth. Or

you could check the depth first by using a powerful handheld sounder, like the Polar Vision, that will give you a depth reading even through foggy ice. The latter option is obviously the easiest and quickest. If you don't have a Polar Vision, you may be able to get a reading by placing the transducer of an ordinary depth finder right on the ice. With either unit, be sure to pour a little water on the ice before sounding.

If you watch a jigging expert work a piece of walleye structure, you might think he's on a "search-and-destroy" mission. He may drill dozens and sometimes even hundreds of holes to find the fish.

Let's say you're working an 18- to 24-foot break. You would probably want to drill a line of holes at 18, 20, 22 and 24 feet. That way, you can work your way around the structure at one depth, then jump out to the next depth and do the same. The fish may be in the deeper holes in midday and then move shallower for the evening bite. Your holes are already there and you won't have to start drilling at sunset and risk spooking the fish off the structure.

A supersharp power auger is a must when doing that much drilling. My personal favorite is the Strikemaster Laser auger. Its unique curved blade cuts a hole in half the time that it takes any other auger I've used. And unlike most other augers, it will easily open up an old hole, saving you even more drilling time.

Ice fishing for walleyes can be a challenge, but there are some big rewards. Those trophy-size walleyes that played hard-to-get all summer are a lot more active in winter, because the lake's food supply is at its annual low and the fish are hungry. In many lakes, your odds of catching a trophy double or even triple in winter. Thinking about that should help keep you warm.

TIPS FOR WINTER WALLEYES

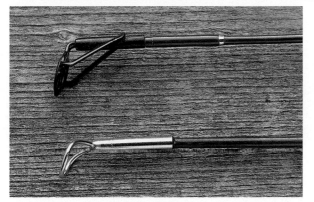

Replace the tip of your jigging rod with a fly rod tiptop (bottom). Less ice will accumulate on this type of guide, and the ice that does form can easily be flicked off with your finger.

Carry your day's supply of minnows in a lockable plastic bag, which is kept in your pocket. This way, you don't have to lug a minnow bucket around, and the bait stays fresh all day.

Use a handheld GPS to return to walleye spots you marked in the summer. Be sure to punch in the landing before you go out, in case a snowstorm develops and you lose sight of shore.

Check the depth with a "flashlight" type sounder. Carry a spray bottle to squirt a little saltwater on the ice, place the face of the sounder in the water and press the button to get a reading.

Use a flasher with a backlit dial for night fishing. Without some type of light, you won't be able to read the depth on the flasher face. Another option: rig up a small battery-powered light to shine on the dial.

Tip a jigging lure with the head of a minnow. Simply hook the bait through the head and pinch off the rest of the body. The added scent often makes a big difference.

PLANING FOR WALLEYES

by Dave Mull

If you have any doubts about the effectiveness of planer-board fishing, consider this: Gary Parsons is the all-time leading money winner on the pro walleye circuit, and most of his wins came by trolling with planer boards.

"It's all a matter of improving your odds," said Parsons of his planer-board approach. "Once you know the right depth and the type of presentation the walleyes want, you just set up a trolling grid so you thoroughly cover the fish zone both horizontally and vertically. Then you simply fine-tune the whole setup until you're concentrating the lures around as many fish as possible."

Sounds simple, but it's not. Whoever thinks trolling is a "no-brainer" method hasn't fished with Parsons. He is constantly adjusting his boat speed, changing lures, varying depths and watching the electronics.

"Trolling is a great way to fish because your lure is in the water 100 percent of the time and you can easily target suspended walleyes," Parsons said. "Planers make it possible to put more lures in the water and cover more area. They're also a must when the fish are shallow, because trolling over them would cause them to spook."

Parsons learned to use planer boards on Wisconsin's massive Lake Winnebago. Throughout the year, the walleyes there often hang over big mud flats, and are susceptible to well-presented crankbaits. Parsons believes these fish relate to mayfly and other insect hatches, feeding on the baitfish that follow the bugs.

Basic Types of Planer Boards

Parsons leans toward "in-line" planer boards. These lightweight devices attach directly to the fishing line. They're small and easy to store. Some designs pop off the line when a fish hits, then float so you can pick them up after the fish has been landed. Other planers stay attached to the line when the fish strikes, but turn in such a way that they offer little resistance during the fight. You reel the board to the rod tip, detach it, and land the fish.

Skis plane to the side on a cord, rather than attach to your fishing line. The cord is elevated on a mast so that it doesn't drag in the water, and the boards are retrieved with large reels mounted on the mast. Your fishing line is attached to the cord with a release device. A strike trips the release and you can fight the fish on a free line.

"If I'm fishing alone or working specific structure, I'll use the in-line planers" said Parsons. "If I'm using lead-core line or fishing huge flats, I'll use a ski and mast. Skis give you wider coverage and won't ride too low from the weight of the lead-core. But skis are hard for one person to operate by himself, so you'll need a partner."

In-Line Planer

Ski-Type Planer

Gearing Up for Planer-Board Fishing

"Filling a trolling grid is easier if you use the same kind of reels and the same line," Parsons says. "Identical line on each rod creates the same amount of drag in the water. Then, your only variable is the lures themselves.

"The thinner the line, the better. Thicker diameter lines have more water resistance, which impedes lures from diving. That's why I've switched to FireLine. It gives me 30 percent more depth from a big-lipped crankbait than I'd get with mono. All my reels are spooled with 10-pound FireLine. The line doesn't stretch a bit, so it transmits the vibrations of the lure, making it easy to see when it's running right and when it's not, even when you've got 200 feet of line out."

Parsons uses a large capacity level-wind reel with a line-counter that enables him to precisely measure the amount of line he lets out. That way, he can return to precisely the same depth when he catches a fish. He prefers 7-foot, medium-heavy rods with a light tip that wiggles easily to show the vibration of the bait. When the tip stops vibrating, he knows the bait is fouled.

Depth control is accomplished by selecting crankbaits that run at different levels and varying the amount of line used. Another depth-control option is the use of Snap Weights (p.77). Experience has taught Parsons how much line it takes for specific lures to reach certain depths, but he doesn't try to be overly precise.

"There are just too many variables to say that if you let out 80 yards of line with a No. 7 Shad Rap, you'll be fishing 12 feet deep," said Parsons. "It will be close to 12 feet, but it might be 11 and it might be 13. What matters to me is that the grid is covered. I want lures spread throughout the fish zone."

For precise information on how deep various crankbaits run, Parsons recommends the book "Precision Trolling" by Dr. Steven Holt. Using scuba gear, Holt measured the running depths of most popular crankbaits and compiled a graph, such as the one below, for each.

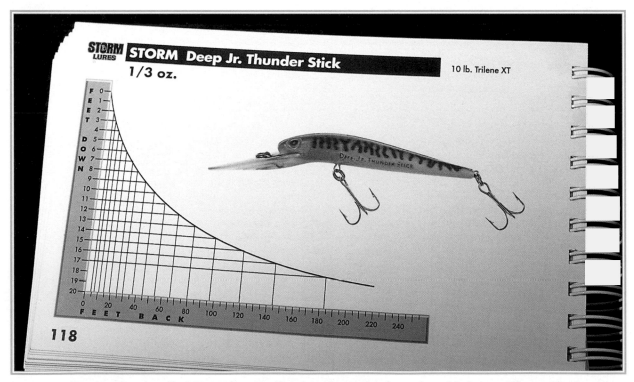

Parsons relies on a book called "Precision Trolling" to determine how deep his lures will run. The book includes charts that plot the running depths of different crankbaits and minnowbaits when trolled at varying distances behind the boat. This chart presents information for the Strom Deep Jr. ThunderStick trolled on 10-pound Trilene XT. When trolled 64 feet back, for example, the lure runs at 11.5 feet. When trolled 120 feet back, it runs at 15 feet.

Let out the desired amount of line as indicated by the line counter on the reel. When no weight is added, you'll normally want to let out 125 to 150 feet.

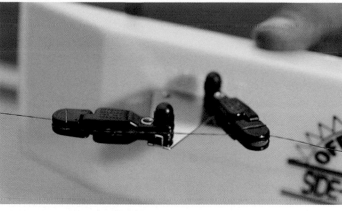

Point the right-side board in the direction you're trolling with the releases facing you, and pinch the line into both releases. When using FireLine, loop the line around one jaw of each release to prevent slippage.

Set the board in the water and let it plane out by releasing line from your reel; lock the reel to stop the board.

Put the rod in a rod holder so it is nearly vertical. Line dragging in the water will keep the board from planing. Set the left-side board in the same manner.

Watch the boards closely. If one of them dips or starts to move inward, you probably have a fish.

Reel in the board so your partner can pinch the releases to remove the board from the line. Keep the boat moving so no slack develops while the board is being removed.

Reel in the fish with a steady pull; do not pump it. Keep the boat running straight so the fish does not cross your other lines and tangle in them.

Lure Selection

Parsons uses long-bodied minnowbaits for most planer-board trolling, but there are times when he switches to deeper-bodied shad-type baits.

When the water is below 50°F, he prefers small-lipped, shallow-running minnowbaits, which have only a slight wobble. At temperatures from 50 to 60°F, he favors baits with a larger lip and moderate wobble. Above 60°F, he may go with big-lipped, wide-wobbling baits, but he'll also experiment with baits that have less action.

For open-water trolling, Parsons leans heavily toward blue-and-silver crankbaits because they match the color of most open-water forage fish. He likes a splash of red or orange for extra attraction. Other favorites include rainbow trout and, for deep water, green and chartreuse with an orange belly.

If crankbaits aren't working, Parsons' next choice is a spinner rig baited with a nightcrawler. He likes spinners with oversized blades and a double-hook crawler harness. When hooking on the crawler, be sure to leave a little extra line between the hooks so the worm can stretch out.

(1)Bomber Long A, (2) Reef Runner, (3) Hot n' Tot, (4) Shad Rap, (5) Rattlin' Rogue, (6) ThunderStick.

TIPS FOR PLANER BOARD FISHING

Loosen your drag enough that a fish can easily pull out line, and then put on the clicker. This compensates for the non-stretch line, preventing hook tear-outs.

If you don't have a line-counter reel, keep track of the amount of line you're using by counting the number of passes of the level-wind bar.

Use Triple-Grip hooks to reduce the number of fish lost during the fight. With non-stretch line, the mouth often tears a little, and an ordinary hook may slip out of the hole.

Controlling Your Depth

When you're trolling in water deeper than your crankbait can reach on its own, Parsons recommends using Snap Weights, sinkers that attach to your line with a pinch-on clip. They are ideal for use with crankbaits because they can be attached far ahead of the lure. This way, you can keep the weight riding well off bottom while the lure is ticking bottom. With an ordinary sinker only a few feet ahead of the crankbait, both the sinker and lure would be bumping bottom, leading to more snags.

Snap Weights also work well for following irregular structure, because they allow you to fish with a shorter line, giving you more control over the path of your baits.

A 1-ounce Snap Weight will add 5 to 15 feet of depth, depending on your bait and trolling speed. You may need 6 ounces of weight or more to get down 50 feet. When using in-line planers, however, Parsons seldom uses weights of more than 3 ounces because the boards will not support them.

The only sure way to know how much weight is needed is to experiment. If you see fish suspended 10 feet off bottom, for example, clip on a Snap Weight and let out line until you feel the bait bump bottom. Then reel in 10 or 20 feet, try fishing for awhile, and reel in a little more. When you catch a fish, note the reading on your line-counter so you can return to the same depth.

Let out about 150 feet of line, and then clip on a Snap Weight, looping the line around one jaw (inset) to prevent slippage.

THE "BOTTOM-UP" SNAP-WEIGHT METHOD

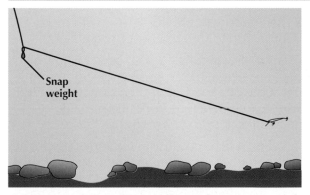

Snap weight

Continue to let out line until your bait starts to tick bottom. If the fish are on the bottom, reel in just a few turns. If the fish are suspended, reel up a little at a time until you start catching them.

When you hook a fish, reel in line until you reach the Snap Weight. Then, unsnap it from the line and continue reeling. Be sure to keep tension on the fish while unsnapping the weight.

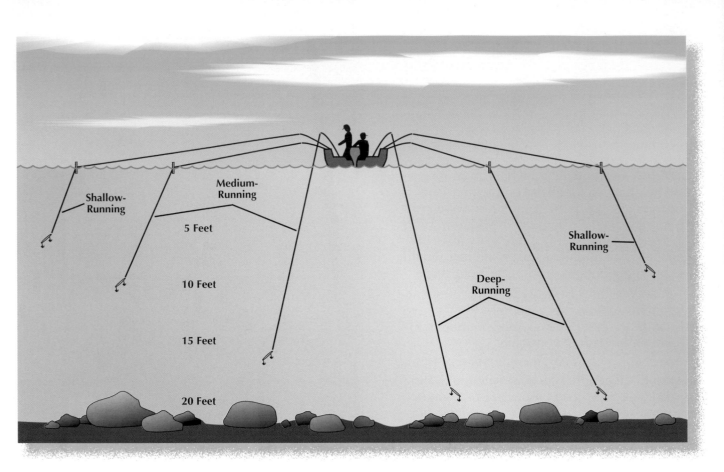

Shallow-
Running

Medium-
Running

5 Feet

10 Feet

15 Feet

20 Feet

Deep-
Running

Shallow-
Running

Planer-Board Strategies

When the fish are suspended, Parsons covers as much water and as many depths as possible. He and a fishing partner usually start with six crankbaits (in states where that many lines are legal). Four lines are fished on boards while two trail directly behind the boat. The outside pair of boards pull shallow-running crankbaits; the inner pair, medium- or deep-running models. The two lines directly behind the boat (as much as 150 yards) also get medium- or deep-running cranks. Depending on the water depth, Snap Weights may be needed to get the baits down to the fish zone.

Once set up, Parsons lets the spread go for 10 minutes or so, then starts changing lures. If one line catches a fish, he resets it with the same bait at the same depth. If it catches another fish within a short time, he'll duplicate the presentation with two other rods. "Before long, you might be running six identical baits," Parsons explains.

All the lures in your spread should be compatible, meaning that they work well at the same speed. "Normally I'll start with all cranks," Parsons says. "I don't start using live bait until I've established a pattern with

cranks. Then I'll fool with other baits on one line to see if something works better. If I'm running spinners and live bait, all my lines usually have them. It's hard to get optimum performance from most crankbaits at spinner speed. On occasion, I'll use small-lipped cranks along with baited spinners because they work well at slow speed."

"When the spread is set, I troll in 'S' curves. That makes the lures on the outside of the turn run faster and those on the inside, slower. Sometimes the fish will show a preference for a specific speed, providing you with more information to fine tune your presentation."

Another way to vary your speed is to troll with the wind. That way, you speed up from the surge of a wave and slow down when the wave passes. Parsons normally runs his crankbaits at .8 to 1.5 miles per hour.

When a fish hits, it usually hooks itself. The key is sharp hooks. Parsons hand sharpens the hooks on all the crankbaits in his arsenal. "My hook-up rate is 95 percent," he says. He has found that Mustad's Triple-Grip hooks, which have an inward bend, greatly reduce the number of fish that shake off when he's reeling them in.

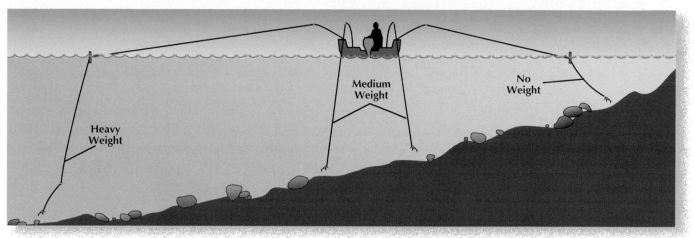

Work a slope by running an unweighted line on a planer on the inside line, a heavily weighted line on a planer board on the outside and two moderately weighted lines straight behind the boat.

Parsons believes that the boat often herds fish right into the path of lures and baits trailing behind planer boards. In other words, fish that spook to the side when the boat passes over them are moving right into the path of the lures. Although herding is most common in shallower water, the phenomenon occurs with suspended fish, too – usually on calm days.

"Sometimes we catch fish on the inside lines with nothing coming on the outside lines," Parsons notes. "The boat seems to move fish out of its pathway, and the nearest baits get hit. When this happens, I duplicate the depth and presentation with the outside lines, and move them to within three feet of the inside lines."

Although planers are used mostly on flat expanses, they can also be used on slopes. In some cases, the fish are shallow, holding at a specific depth along the shoreline. Then Parsons keeps his boat in deeper water to prevent spooking the shallow fish and runs his baits over them with planer boards.

Parsons believes a GPS unit is indispensable on big flats – especially when there are no visible landmarks on shore. A GPS not only takes him back to the place he caught fish the day before, it helps him pinpoint schools of fish.

"Suspended fish are moving constantly," Parsons points out. "A GPS will help you stay with them." When he catches the first fish, he immediately hits the quick-save

Waypoint patterns show size of walleye school.

button to store that waypoint. As he catches more fish, he stores additional waypoints. When he stops catching fish, he trolls back to those waypoints to see if the fish are still there.

"You're not going in a straight line between waypoints," Parsons explains. "You're trolling off to the side to determine the size of the school. Eventually you'll have a pretty good idea of how big the school is and how the fish are moving."

Planer boards are not necessary in the majority of walleye fishing situations. But when walleyes are suspended, scattered over large flats or spooking from your boat, planers can make the difference between a disastrous trip and a banner day.

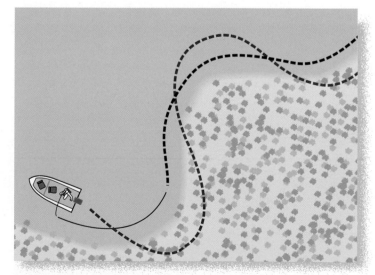

Follow irregular structure by cutting inside the contour on inside turns; outside on outside turns (red line). This way, the lures will stay at a consistent depth (black line) as you troll along the structure.

GIVE A RIP FOR WALLEYES

by Dick Sternberg

Check out northern Minnesota's Lake Winnibigoshish most any summer day and you're likely to see an unusual sight: walleye anglers violently jerking their rods as they motor along. No, they're not trying to shake off weeds. They're rip-jigging.

Also called snap-jigging, this unorthodox technique was popularized by a Minnesotan named Dick (the Griz) Grzywinski more than a decade ago. Then an obscure, part-time fishing guide, Grzywinski had been raising eyebrows on Big Winnie and other northern Minnesota lakes with his routine hundred-plus walleye days. Soon, word of his phenomenal catches began to spread and Grzywinski started to draw attention from the pro-walleye crowd.

The Griz is not a tournament fisherman but, when he started to gain notoriety, he was invited to a charity fishing event attended by dozens of the Midwest's top anglers. He and his guests lapped the field with a catch of 97 walleyes and 54 northerns – in a 6-hour trip!

Several top pros started following the Griz on his excursions to Winnie, but nobody could seem to pick up on the technique. Most of them soon gave up out of frustration and embarrassment.

Here's how one of the pros described his experience: "There he (the Griz) was, weaving between 30 or 40 boats along a shallow rock spine, catching 10 walleyes for every one in all the other boats combined. So I figure, the fish are really in there. If he can catch 'em like that, I'll really nail 'em on 4-pound test with a 1/64-ounce jig and a leech. Boy, was I wrong!"

As difficult as the technique is to master, it's even harder to explain. When Grzywinski describes what he does, he really doesn't pin down the details. "After a while, ya just kinda get a feel for it," he says.

The difficulty of describing the technique probably explains why it's being used successfully by only a handful of accomplished walleye anglers, and why it has never really received significant press coverage.

A collection of Polaroids from Griz's scrapbook documents his consistent rip-jigging success.

Rip-jigging enables you to fish through some types of weeds, such as cabbage. The sharp jerks shatter the leaves.

Understanding the Technique

Being one of the Griz's fishing buddies, I've spent a lot of time observing his rip-jigging technique and discussing its intricacies with him. While I don't profess to be an expert, I have rip-jigged my way to some outstanding catches, usually after everything else I tried failed. My best advice for someone who wants to learn to rip-jig: *Start with the basic principles of jig fishing, then do just the opposite.*

Let me explain:

•Standard jig-trolling procedure is to back-troll very slowly. Rip-jigging involves trolling forward at two or three times normal jig-trolling speed.

•Usual jig-trolling strategy is to keep your line as close to vertical as possible. When rip-jigging, you toss the lure far behind the boat.

•In standard jig trolling, you twitch the jig lightly. In rip-jigging, you jerk it violently.

•Ordinarily, you keep your jig bumping bottom, twitching it and allowing it to settle back. But in rip-jigging, you keep the jig off bottom, never allowing it to touch.

•You normally twitch a jig, then maintain a taut line as it sinks. In rip-jigging, you intentionally throw some slack into the line as the jig sinks.

•The usual way of detecting a jig strike is to intently feel for a subtle tap as the jig is sinking. In rip-jigging, you often don't feel the tap; you just hook the fish on the next snap of the rod.

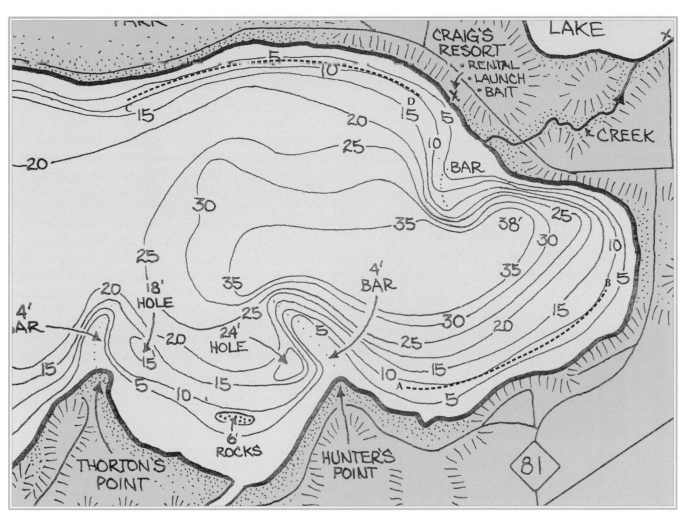

Good rip-jigging locations include the long breaklines from A to B and C to D.

When & Where to Rip-Jig

Primarily a warm water technique, rip-jigging can be effective well into the fall. When the water temperature drops below 50°F, however, walleyes may refuse to chase a fast-moving jig.

Prime rip-jigging water is less than 15 feet deep, with long, subtle breaklines, but it's possible to rip-jig in water as deep as 25 feet. "Most people think there's no structure where I do my rip-jigging," Grzywinski says. "They don't realize I'm following a gradual break. You see guys weaving back and forth along the break, but I keep my boat at a precise depth – exactly where the fish are."

"Lots of times I find walleyes around 7 feet, even on calm, sunny days. There are a lot more fish in shallow water than people think – and the shallow ones are the biters."

The bottom where Grzywinski does most of his rip-jigging is sandy, sometimes with light weed growth. But you can also rip-jig over rock reefs or weedbeds, particularly cabbage or coontail. Just run the jig right over the weed tops and rip it hard when you feel it catch a weed. "Walleyes will come right out of the weeds and blast it," the Griz explains. "They think its a minnow trying to get away."

"Time of day doesn't seem to matter – I catch 'em all day long. Sometimes the best bite is right in the middle of the day."

Rip-jigging has an unparalleled triggering effect on walleyes. Like most predator fish, they will focus on a baitfish swimming abnormally, while ignoring an entire school swimming in unison. So it's not surprising that they find it hard to resist an erratically darting jig. Their propensity for picking out the odd baitfish also explains the technique's effectiveness in late summer, when the glut of young-of-the-year forage fish slows walleye action in most waters.

The Rip-Jigging Technique

Always troll forward into the wind, either directly or at an angle. "I see lots of guys trying to backtroll and rip-jig," says Grzywinski. "That might work when it's calm, but not on a windy day. The waves go right over their heads when they backtroll that fast."

A drift sock off the bow makes boat control much easier.

When it's choppy, the Griz clips a drift-sock on a 3-foot rope clipped to his bow eye. The drift sock stabilizes the bow, so the wind won't swing it around when he trolls forward. With the short rope, the sock will trail back under the boat, but won't foul in the motor.

It's a slick system; not only will you stay dry, you'll enjoy a much smoother ride.

Ironically, rip-jigging is much harder to learn for an accomplished jig fisherman than for a novice. "Women seem to do a lot better at it than men," Grzywinski notes.

My first few rip-jigging attempts were a disaster. Even though I was sitting next to the Griz, observing his every move and trying to duplicate it, he was doing the "ten-to-one" number on me. But after a few embarrassing trips, I finally discovered my mistake: I wasn't throwing enough slack into the line, so my jig didn't have the erratic action of the Griz's.

For a long-time jig fisherman, it's very difficult to break the habit of keeping your line taut as the jig sinks. You must learn to snap your rod forward with a sidearm motion, then immediately drop it back to the starting position before snapping again. This procedure is easy for a novice, but very unnatural for a veteran jigger.

Returning the rod to the initial position is also important for another reason: it puts your arm in position for a strong hookset.

The other difficult part of rip-jigging is gauging the right amount of line. "Ya got to learn how far back to toss the jig for different water depth," the Griz explained. The idea is to keep your jig as close to bottom as possible without making a contact. As a general rule, your line length should be 4 to 5 times the water depth, although you may need a little more on a windy day to make up for line bow. The only

HOW TO RIP-JIG

Troll into the wind and cast the jig out behind the boat. The length of the cast should be about five times the depth of the water.

Snap the rod sharply just before the jig touches the bottom. You'll have to experiment to determine the proper timing.

sure way to determine the right amount of line, however, is to experiment. If you're picking up weeds or debris, shorten up your line.

The Griz swears by his own hand-tied, chicken-feather jigs. "Takes me an hour to tie one," he grumbles. "But it's worth the trouble – the wiggling feathers drive the fish crazy."

"If the fish are bitin', ya don't even need a minnow – just a plain jig. White or chartreuse – don't make much difference. When it's windy, I like a quarter-ounce; otherwise, I'll use an eighth."

On a trip to North Dakota's Lake Sakakawea a few years back, Grzywinski made a believer of some local guides by badly outfishing them with an unbaited Griz Jig. When one of them didn't show up the next day, his friend explained, "he went out to the farm to catch some chickens."

Another of Grzywinski's favorites is the Northland Fireball jig, tipped with a fathead minnow hooked through the eyes. "Fireballs are easier for my customers to use," he notes. "You hook more fish because of the short shank."

Grzywinski prefers a 7-foot, fast-tip spinning rod for rip-jigging. The long rod helps him snap the jig with less effort, and makes it easier to take up the slack when setting the hook. He normally spools up with 8- to 10-pound Trilene XT. Lighter or softer line simply won't stand up to the violent jerking. Even tough, heavy line must be changed frequently because the rodtip frays it.

THE GRIZ'S FAVORITE JIGS

When the fish are striking short, Grzywinski uses a (1) Northland Fireball with a fathead hooked through the eye sockets. When they're moderately aggressive, he prefers a (2) Griz Jig with a fathead hooked through the lips. When they're highly aggressive, he uses a (3) plain Griz Jig.

Rip-jigging is definitely one of the most difficult walleye techniques to master, but it is something every walleye angler should have in his arsenal. It will trigger walleyes to bite when nothing else is working.

Drop your rod back to the starting position immediately after the snap. This throws slack into the line and causes the jig to sink freely. Continue repeating the snap and drop.

If you feel anything different, set the hook. Should a fish grab the jig as it's sinking, you may not feel a strike, but when you snap the rod, you automatically set the hook.

TURN WEEDS INTO WALLEYES

by James Churchill

The average walleye fisherman believes that weeds are something to be avoided. But that's a serious mistake, according to Greg Bohn, well-known fishing guide and tackle manufacturer from Hazelhurst, Wisconsin. Bohn knows that weeds provide secure cover and a good source of food for many kinds of gamefish – including walleyes.

Relying heavily on baits that his company manufactures, Bohn and his clients boat more than 3,000 walleyes in an average year, and a good share of them come from weedy cover.

Bohn specializes in extracting walleyes from exactly the kinds of spots that most walleye fisherman shy away from. "I especially like to fish small, shallow weedy lakes early in the season," Bohn explains. "They warm up the fastest and activate the fish!"

In spring, Bohn favors lakes that have shallow bays on the north side. These bays warm up sooner than bays on the south, because prevailing southerly winds push warmer surface water into them. Weeds start growing earliest there too, attracting baitfish and, in turn, walleyes.

How Wind Affects Early-Season Water Temperature

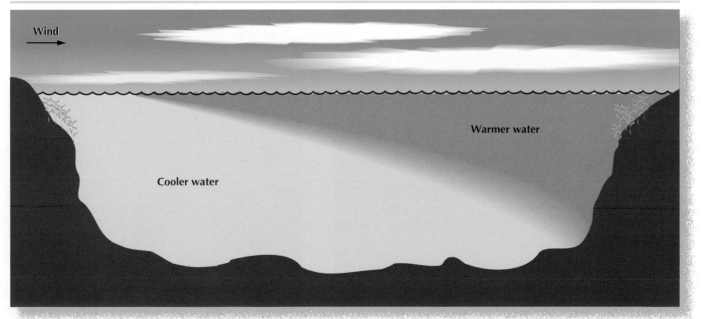

On a sunny day in spring, the top few inches of a lake may be 10 degrees warmer than the water below. The wind pushes this water along and it accumulates along the downwind shore, explaining why the water temperature there is so much warmer than in the main lake. Conversely, an offshore wind pushes the warm water away from the shore and cold water wells up to replace it, so the temperature along the upwind shore is colder than in the main lake.

Fishing the Weeds in Spring

Bohn with a hefty weed walleye.

On a recent spring day, we headed out to check one of Bohn's favorite lakes, which has three shallow bays along the north and northwest shores. We put the boat in the water and immediately began checking these bays for newly emerging weed growth. In the northwest bay, Bohn found the weedbed he was looking for and dropped a marker buoy. At the other end of the bed, he dropped another. He had located an emerging patch of short, green "broadleaf cabbage," less than 10-inches tall.

The weedbed was in 6 feet of water but was adjacent to a drop-off, which sloped down to 20 feet. Bohn marked the outer edge of the bed with two more buoys. Next, he proceeded on to the other bays, where he marked two more weedbeds.

We then headed back to the first marked weedbed. "By now the walleyes that may have spooked on our first pass should have settled down," Bohn explained. "The first time you fish a lake, you almost have to run right over the weeds to see them. Then, you have to give the fish a little time to recover. Of course, if we had landed here later in the day with the right sun, we could have spotted the weeds with Polaroid sunglasses without running over them. But then we would have missed the morning bite."

THE TOP "WALLEYE WEEDS"

Canada waterweed grows in long strands like coontail, but the strands are smaller in diameter and the individual leaves are shorter and broader.

Broadleaf cabbage may grow in water as much as 14 feet deep. The leaves are more than an inch wide and the flowering heads often stick out of the water.

Bohn cut the big engine about 200 feet from the weedbed and used the transom-mount electric to move slowly closer. He rigged his rod with a ¹/₁₆-ounce, round-head chartreuse-and-orange jig with an oversized hook (size 2) tipped with a 2½-inch fathead minnow.

For this type of fishing, Bohn uses a 7-foot, one-piece graphite spinning rod with an extra-fast tip and an open-face reel spooled with 6-pound mono. He believes you need the sensitivity of a graphite rod and he designs and markets his own "Stinger" rods that are rated for ¹/₃₂- to ¼-ounce lures and 4- to 10-pound mono.

Bohn casts well into the weedbed. Later in the season, after the weeds get thick, it will be impossible to work a jig through the bed, but now the jig snakes between the plants and back to the boat with ease. He retrieves the jig with a smooth, swimming motion. "Try to hop a jig in the weeds and you will most likely hang up," he explains.

If he starts hanging up too much, Bohn switches to his own weedless jig, called a "Timber Jig," which has a frayed-cable-type weed guard. This guard is extremely flexible, but he recommends a strong hookset. "Hit 'em as hard as you can," he says. "You won't break 6-pound mono!"

His strategy worked and the bites came. By the time we had fished all three weedbeds, we had boated a two-man limit of walleyes.

Bohn offered an explanation for our early spring success. "I settled for cabbage weed,

(1) ¹/₁₆-ounce round-head jig tipped with fathead minnow, (2) ¹/₁₆-ounce Timber Jig tipped with fathead.

although I was looking for a weed named Elodea. It's properly called Canada water-weed, but I call it walleye weed because walleyes love it. Find it and you've found walleyes. Elodea comes up early in the spring and is often found near inlet streams. Besides cabbage and Elodea, other preferred weeds are coontail and sand grass. Bulrush, water lilies and cattails aren't as good, but they'll sometimes hold walleyes if their favorite weeds are scarce."

Sand grass, properly called Chara, often blankets the bottom in depths as great as 35 feet. It has a skunky odor and is sometimes called skunkgrass.

Coontail grows in dense masses that are not rooted. It is commonly found in depths as great as 35 feet.

One of Bohn's classic weed-walleye haunts is a broadleaf cabbage-weed patch. In summer, he spots cabbage beds by looking for the seed pods that stick out of the water. In deep, clear water, however, the cabbage may not grow all the way to the surface. It sometimes tops out as much as 6 feet beneath the water.

Fishing the Weeds in Summer

When Bohn and I got together again in midsummer, the weeds were well developed on all the lakes in the area. In fact, the small lake that we had fished earlier in the spring was so weed-choked it couldn't be fished. Bohn instead chose a 1,000-acre lake containing several varieties of weeds.

After launching the boat, we headed for two mid-lake weedbeds. They were hard to see and were bypassed by most anglers. All that showed above the surface were a few seed pods from the broadleaf cabbage patch.

"In midsummer, walleyes will almost always go to an offshore weedbed to feed," Bohn

revealed. "On this lake the submerged weeds grow only about three feet tall because the water clarity is low. So when you see them sticking above the surface in mid-lake, you know you're on a shallow hump."

A glance at the hydrographic map of the lake showed that we were, in fact, on a flat-topped hump surrounded by deep water. "I guarantee that walleyes will be working this weedbed", Bohn said confidently. "Let's try it."

A brisk wind was blowing whitecaps across the hump as Bohn outlined our approach. "In this situation, we could drift across the top of the hump and throw jigs. But this particular hump is too shallow, and we'd probably spook the fish. We could also anchor or hold upwind and cast jigs across the top of the hump. This might take some fish, but I'd rather go downwind of the hump and anchor, then cast into the wind. You'll hang up less this way, because you'll be pulling the jig in the same direction the weeds are lying after being pushed downwind by the waves. The wind also creates a current over the top of the hump, and feeding fish face upstream, just like they do on a river," Bohn explained. "The jig will come at them from the direction they expect food!"

Bohn recommends using as light a jig as possible. A 1/8-ounce jig is about the lightest you can cast into a stiff breeze, and sometimes it takes a 1/4-ounce. Even so, you may have to cast sidearm to keep the lure low enough to punch into the wind.

The jig must also be heavy enough to reach any fish that are holding deep along the sides of the hump. Bohn uses a weedless jig or a weighted weedless hook that can be worked slowly without hanging up. He tips the jig or hook with a leech, which he feels is the best midsummer bait. Leeches stay on the hook and walleyes relish them.

Bohn also uses slip bobbers to fish mid-lake weedbeds. The trick is to use enough split shot to nearly sink the bobber; this way, it is less affected by wind or current and a walleye can pull it under with little resistance. For bait, he uses a lively leech on a size 6 gold Aberdeen hook or a 1/8-ounce jig head. He sets the bobber to a depth where it will carry the bait right over the weed tops, then casts into the wind or anchors on the side of the hump and casts across wind.

"Deep weedbeds are also midsummer hotspots," Bohn points out. "I call these deep weeds, which consist mainly of short sand grass in 25 to 30 feet of water, the 'lake carpet.' Walleyes, especially the bigger, nonaggressive ones, often suspend right over the top of the lake carpet, or they may even burrow into it if it's thick enough."

Bohn contends that the carpet is usually unfished. The weeds don't show up on most depth finders and fishermen don't realize the fish are there. He works these sand-grass beds with a jig and leech, drifting along while the bait just brushes the weed tops.

Bohn always wears polarized sunglasses because they make it easier to spot holes in the weed patches. Most often, the openings result from rock piles or a clean sand bottom that will not support weed growth, so they're ideal walleye spots. Bohn fishes these holes by holding close to them or right over them and jigging vertically, or by using a slip-bobber rig set to fish just off bottom. After fishing a hole, he resets the bobber and fishes the weed tops.

If the cabbage is less than six feet tall, Bohn fishes it by drifting or slow-trolling with a slip-sinker rig and a plain hook or floating jig head, both weedless. He sets the length of the snell so the floating jig works through the upper layer of weeds.

"Weed-walleye fishing can be great in fall," Bohn claims, "but the weed situation is a lot different than in spring and summer. Most of the weeds have died, so the fish have moved out to deep water. If you can find some bright green weeds, though, you're almost guaranteed to catch walleyes."

Bohn switches back to a jig and minnow in fall, but he often uses a bigger bait, like a 3- to 4-inch redtail chub. The natural forage in

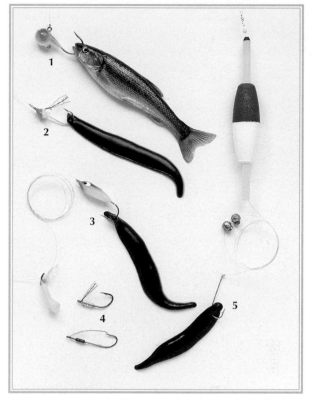

(1) ⅛-ounce Fireball Jig tipped with redtail chub, (2) ⅛-ounce Timber Jig tipped with leech, (3) slip-sinker rig with floating jig head and leech, (4) weedless hooks, (5) slip-bobber rig and leech on size 6 gold Aberdeen hook.

the lake has grown over the summer, so the walleyes are looking for larger food.

Catching weed walleyes isn't easy. You need some specialized gear and a precise presentation. But once you learn the proper techniques, you'll enter a world of walleye fishing that most anglers never see.

TIPS FOR SUMMERTIME WEED WALLEYES

Retrieve with the "grain" of the weeds. Determine which way the wind is pushing the weeds and then cast directly into the wind to minimize hang-ups.

When fishing in dense weeds, replace the egg sinker or walking sinker on your slip-sinker rig with a bullet sinker, which slides through weeds without fouling.

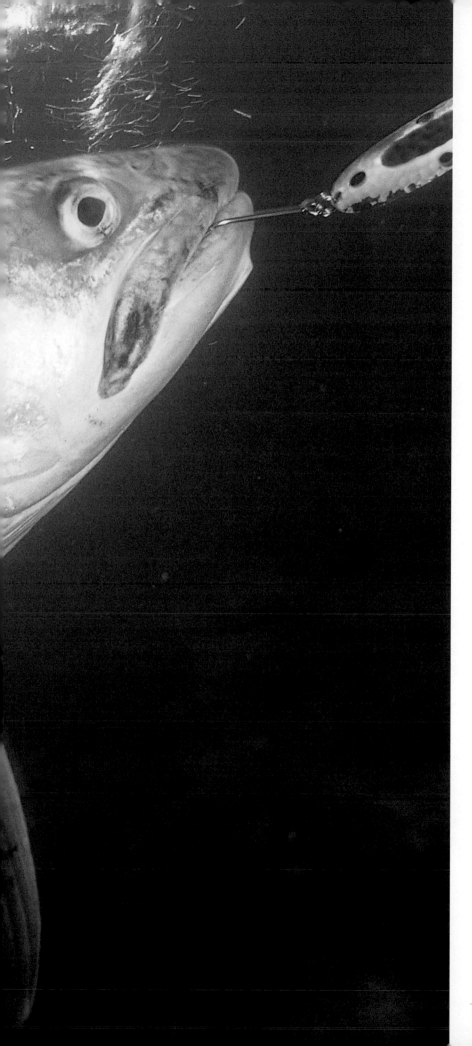

Trout & Salmon

Widespread stocking has put these explosive fighters within reach of more anglers than ever before.

Vertical casting with a heavy spoon fooled this nice laker.

VERTICAL "CASTING" FOR DEEP-WATER LAKERS

by Dick Sternberg

"Listen carefully," I instructed my friend, Bill Diedrich, as he was about to try my newly discovered lake trout method. "This is an extremely complicated technique, and you've got to do everything exactly right."

"OK, so what do I do?" he asked.

"Drop your spoon to the bottom and reel it back up," I replied, trying to keep a straight face. "Like I said, it's really complex – sort of like vertical casting."

Diedrich and I were fishing on Selwyn Lake, on the border of Saskatchewan and the Northwest Territories. It was mid-July and the trout were deep, from 60 to well over 100 feet. Being veteran lake trout anglers, we knew we could easily get down to the fish by trolling with downriggers or heavy weights, or by bouncing leadhead jigs on the bottom. But downriggers take away from the thrill of hooking the fish yourself, and heavy weights take away from the fight. So we were doing some jigging, with sporadic success, when I started

telling him about my newly discovered "vertical casting" method. He sounded intrigued, so we decided to try it.

It didn't take long to make Diedrich a believer. As he was reeling up on his third drop, his rod doubled over. "Good fish," he muttered, struggling to gain a little line. When I looked at his rodtip and saw the slow, throbbing motion, I knew it was more than a "good" one.

Fifteen minutes later, I slipped the net under a 44-incher that we estimated to weigh 37 pounds. Not bad for maybe two minutes of vertical casting.

In a three-day period, Diedrich and I took nearly 600 lakers using the vertical casting technique, firmly establishing it as a permanent part of our lake-trout repertoire.

On an earlier trip to Selwyn, Gord Wallace, proprietor of Selwyn Lake Lodge, introduced me to his brand of vertical casting. He simply motored out a few hundred yards from the lodge, dropped a heavy spoon down to the bottom, jigged it several times, and then rapidly reeled it back up.

Sometimes the fish hit when he was jigging, but more often, they grabbed the spoon when he was reeling up, often just a few feet beneath the boat. In a 2-hour period, I saw Wallace land at least 20 trout from 5 to 12 pounds and one 25-pounder, all on a light spinning outfit and what appeared to be a red-and-white Dardevle.

The Vertical-Casting Technique

Fishing alongside Wallace, I was trying to mimic his technique, with little success. I found a red-and-white spoon in my tackle box, but evidently wasn't working it the right way. Then Wallace pulled up next to me and tossed me one of his spoons. "Here's my secret bait," he said. "Give it a try." The lure, which I later learned was a Blue Fox Tor-P-

BEST BAITS FOR
VERTICAL CASTING

(1) 2-ounce Krocodile spoon, (2) 1½-ounce Tor-P-Do spoon, (3) size 7 Swedish Pimple, (4) ½-ounce Sonar.

Do spoon, had metal at least twice as thick as the spoon I was using. Weighing 1½ ounces, it also sank twice as fast and had a much faster wobble.

Changing to the Tor-P-Do Spoon immediately paid off; I was catching a trout on every second or third drop. After doing some additional experimenting, I found I could take even more trout by eliminating the jigging altogether and simply dropping the lure down and reeling it up. Cranking up rapidly from the start evidently makes the fish think their meal is getting away, so they swim up and grab it. At one point, I hooked seven trout on seven consecutive drops.

After considerable experimentation, I found some other lures that would work. I caught fish on Luhr-Jensen Krocodiles, Swedish Pimples, Heddon Sonars and Blitz Blades, but nothing outproduced the Tor-P-Do spoon.

Like Wallace, I was using medium-power spinning tackle with 8-pound test monofilament, but I was having problems hooking fish. In water as much as 100 feet deep, line stretch made it difficult to get a solid hookset. Next day, I rigged up a stiff, 7½-foot flippin' stick and a level-wind reel spooled with 30-pound-test Fireline. What a difference! With the extra backbone and absolutely no line stretch, I could feel the lightest peck and get a considerably stronger hookset. My hooking percentage jumped from maybe 50 to more than 70.

Actually, there is a little more to the technique than simply dropping the spoon down and reeling it up. You have to find schools of trout, and that requires good electronics. I've found a Lowrance LMS-350A to be the ideal unit, especially in the remote country where lake trout are often found, because it combines a high-resolution liquid-crystal graph with a GPS. I set the unit up on a portable "blue box" with a motorcycle battery for power. This rig enables me to quickly check points and reefs for schools of trout and, once I locate them, lock in their position with the GPS.

Most of the lake trout schools you find are surprisingly tight, maybe only 15 or 20 feet in diameter. To help stay on top of these schools, carry a marker such as a bleach jug, rigged with enough string to reach bottom. Toss it well off to the side of the school, so it doesn't interfere with your fishing. Then, turn the transom of your boat into the wind, put your motor in reverse and try to hover precisely over the fish.

If you're positioned properly, you'll almost invariably hook up on the first drop. Often, a fish swims up to intercept the spoon, causing the line to go slack long before it reaches bottom. Sometimes you can see trout on the graph coming up to grab the lure. It's sort of like playing a video game; when a line angles up from the bottom to meet one angling down from the top, be ready to set the hook!

I've seen times when vertical casting initiates a feeding frenzy among the entire school. When one fish starts to chase the spoon upward, the rest of the school follows in what is evidently a competitive response. One day, while ripping a spoon toward the surface, my entire graph screen suddenly turned black. Just then, a trout grabbed the spoon about 20 feet from the surface. As I was landing the fish, the blackness near the bottom gradually disappeared, but the black layer near the surface remained. At first, I thought my graph was on the blink. The thought also crossed my mind that the black layer was a school of trout, but that didn't make sense because there were no distinct "hooks".

After this happened a few times, I finally noticed that when the graph was black, the surface was virtually boiling. As the school of trout swam upward, they were burping up thousands of bubbles, which were causing the graph to turn black. Once the school lifted off the bottom, the deep bubbles gradually floated upward, explaining why the blackness near the bottom disappeared.

To release a trout with a minimum of handling, grab the hook with a pair of needle-nose pliers and give it a sharp upward twist. If you have to lift the fish into the boat to unhook it, you lose valuable fishing time and the fish will flop around in the boat, possibly injuring itself.

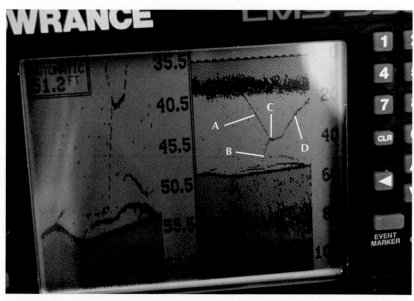

This screen shows (a) spoon dropping down, (b) laker swimming up to grab it, (c) the strike and (d) fish being reeled in.

Most freshwater fish are not capable of chasing a lure from the bottom to the surface in 100 feet of water. The decrease in pressure would cause their swim bladders to blow up like a balloon. But lake trout and other members of the trout family are *physostomous* fish, meaning that they have a duct connecting their esophagus to their swim bladder. This way, they can burp up air as the swim bladder expands, enabling them to freely swim up and down in the water column.

The main drawback to vertical casting is that it tends to work best for smaller-sized trout, those up to about 12 pounds. Big lake trout are not "chasers". They spend most of their time near the bottom, feeding on 14- to 20-inch whitefish and other big forage fish, including smaller lake trout. A small spoon has little appeal to a big lake trout, because chasing a baitfish that size is simply not worth the energy the trout would have to expend.

But there are exceptions, like Diedrich's 37-pounder. And then there was the time we were filming a segment for a nationally syndicated TV show at Selwyn. As the angler was reeling up his spoon and just about to lift it from the water, a giant laker grabbed it. He instinctively reared back to set the hook, instantly snapping his rod in half. As the camera turned to catch the action, the trout headed directly for the bottom. Using the remaining half of his rod, he somehow managed to horse the fish back up and land it. That one weighed 38 pounds.

After experiencing so much success with the vertical casting technique on Selwyn, I was curious to try it out on a lake closer to home. So when my friends Jack Schneider and Dave Funk invited me on a lake trout trip to Saganaga Lake in northeastern Minnesota, I jumped at the chance. Saganaga's lakers see a lot of fishing pressure, so I was anxious to see how "educated" trout would respond.

As we motored out to our spot, Funk spotted the beat-up Tor-P-Do spoon on my line. It was the same one I'd been using on Selwyn. "Whattaya gonna do with that thing?" he asked. "You're not in the Northwest Territories any more."

"We'll see," I said.

I had the rod in my hand and my thumb on the spool as Jack stopped the motor over one of his favorite trout holes. I let the spoon go, felt it hit bottom and started reeling up before Funk had his line in the water. The trout hit almost immediately and within seconds, the 5-pounder was flopping on his boots.

"Damndest thing I've ever seen," he sputtered. "I've been fishing this lake for 10 years and still haven't caught a trout, and you catch one in 30 seconds."

I guess you could argue that vertical casting is a "no-brainer" method. But when you're catching all the fish and the guy next to you is blanking, who's the no-brainer?

TIPS FOR VERTICAL CASTING

Rig a combination sonar-GPS unit on a "Blue Box." The unit will help you find schools of trout and help you return to the precise spots.

Add a 10-foot leader of 14-pound mono when the trout are finicky. Attach the leader to the line with a barrel swivel small enough to reel through the guides, or use a double uni-knot (p.102). Attach the spoon with a Cross-Loc clip.

Bill Diedrich displays his 37-pounder.

Point your transom into the wind and keep the motor idling in reverse to hover over the fish. This way, you can keep your line nearly vertical.

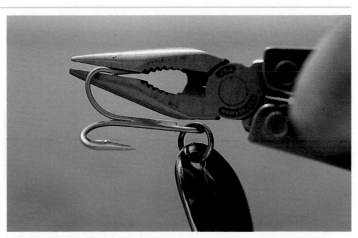

Flatten the barbs on your treble hook to facilitate releasing the fish. When you're on a school, you want to be able to unhook the fish as quickly as possible so you can get your spoon back into the water.

DEEP JIGGING FOR WINTER LAKERS

by Dick Sternberg

The coldwater habits of lake trout make them a favorite target for ice fishermen. While most warmwater gamefish tend to become sluggish in the frigid water, lakers stay active, feeding as heavily as ever. And they seem to fight extra hard in winter; it's not unusual to bring one up to the hole, only to watch helplessly as it power dives right back to the bottom.

There are many similarities between lake trout and walleye fishing. Like walleyes, lakers are structure-oriented, relating to points, humps, saddles and irregular breaklines. They're also found in deep holes and slots. But the structure they inhabit is anywhere from two to four times as deep as that typically used by walleyes.

Although lakers are normally found at depths of 40 to 70 feet during the winter, there are times when they retreat to depths of 100 feet or more. Unlike walleyes, which all tend to run at about the same level, lakers may be caught at a variety of depths. I've taken them in water ranging from 30 to 80 feet deep on the same day.

As in walleye fishing, you must be mobile in order to find the structure that is holding fish. In fact, mobility is even more important because of the variability in depths. Be sure to check the spots where you found trout during the summer months. Unlike most other salmonids, lakers are homebodies, staying in the same vicinity all their lives.

The need for mobility explains why jigging is rapidly catching on among laker addicts. You can jig several holes in the time it takes to set up one bait rig to fish at the right depth.

TYPICAL LAKE TROUT STRUCTURE

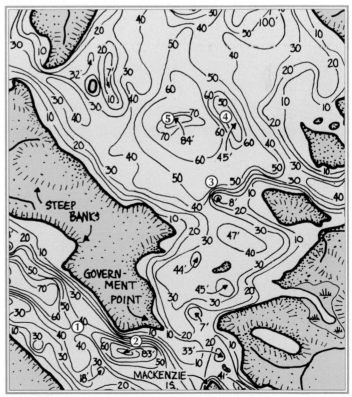

(1) Deep saddle, (2) deep point, (3) irregular breakline, (4) deep hump, (5) deep hole.

Gearing Up for Winter Lakers

You'll need powerful electronics to mark the fish and your lure in deep water. A typical 200 KHZ liquid-crystal, for instance, should have at least 1000 watts of peak-to-peak power. Some of the newer flashers have adequate power for water that deep, but most do not.

HOW TO MAKE A UNI-KNOT SPLICE

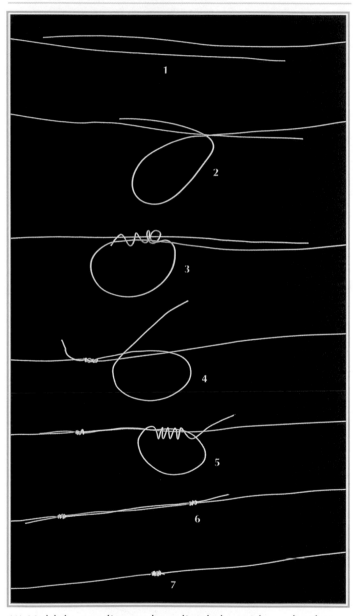

(1) Hold the two lines to be spliced alongside each other so the ends overlap about 6 inches. (2) Form a loop in one line, as shown. (3) Pass the tag end through the loop and wind it around the other line 4 times. (4) Form a loop in the other line. (5) Pass the tag end through the loop and wind it around the opposite line 4 times. (6) Snug up one knot by pulling on the tag end, then snug up the other. (7) Pull on each line to slide the two knots together.

Being able to see your lure and judge how the fish are responding to different actions is even more important in lake trout fishing than in walleye fishing. Lakers love to chase the bait, and you can often tempt a strike by reeling up quickly. I've seen the fish follow a bait from the bottom to just a few feet beneath the ice before taking it. The sight of the bait getting away evidently triggers a reflex strike. Without good electronics, you'd never know what was happening, so a maneuver like this would be impossible.

Setting the hook in deep water can be a big problem in lake trout fishing. If you're fishing in 70 feet of water with monofilament line, you have to contend with about 15 feet of stretch. The only thing you can do is set the hook and start running away from the hole to take up the slack. Veteran trout anglers have traditionally solved the problem by fishing with wire line, but wire kinks very easily and if you don't notice a kink, the line may break when you hook a fish.

Non-stretch "superlines" have solved the problem. They won't kink up, and their extremely thin diameter makes them much less visible than wire line. Another advantage: because they don't stretch, they telegraph bites much better than mono.

Just spool a couple hundred feet of the line (I use 30-pound test) onto a baitcasting reel and use a stiff jigging rod about 3 feet long. The reel should have a level-wind that passes across the spool as you let out line. You may have trouble feeding line on a baitcaster if the level-wind doesn't move as the spool turns. Friction created by the line going through the level-wind at a sharp angle slows the bait's descent, and you're better off getting down to the fish quickly.

Some fishermen tie their jigs directly to the braided line, but I prefer using a 12- to 14-pound-test mono leader. Most trout lakes are extremely clear, and I seem to get more strikes with a leader at least 10 feet long. You can connect the leader to the line with a small barrel swivel, but the swivel may be hard to reel through ice-clogged guides.

Here's a better way to make the connection: use a double Uni-knot, wrapping the mono around the braided line on one end and the braided line around the mono on the other (left). Then pull on the line and the leader to slide the knots together, making a compact knot that tests out at 100 percent. Don't attempt to use a blood knot; it won't work for joining lines of greatly different diameter.

Baits & Lures for Winter Lakers

I use a leadhead jig the majority of the time, but the ones I use are quite a bit different than what are normally considered deepwater trout jigs. I see lots of anglers using 1½-, 2- and even 3-ounce jigs; they assume they need that much weight to get down in water more than 50 feet deep. A heavy jig is a must with stiff wire linc, but with limp, thin diameter braided line, you can easily reach depths of 100 feet with a ½-ounce jig.

A bucktail or feather jig, in white or chartreuse, is hard to beat for winter lakers. Tipping the jig with a 3- to 4-inch shiner minnow, a small cisco or smelt or a strip of cut bait, such as herring or sucker, usually increases the number of strikes. When tipping with cut bait or a good-sized minnow, be sure to use a stinger hook (p.105). If you don't want to tip, use a plain ½-ounce jig head with a 4-inch Berkley Power Tube.

Other good wintertime baits include jigging lures like a size 6 Swedish Pimple and a ½- to 1-ounce airplane jig, which has large wings to make the bait glide. These baits are usually tipped with minnows or cut bait as well. Another productive bait is a vibrating blade, like a ½-ounce Luhr-Jensen Ripple Tail or Heddon Sonar.

A bucktail or feather jig is hard to beat for winter lakers.

(1) ½-ounce feather jig, (2) size 6 Swedish Pimple, (3) Berkley Power Tube on ½-ounce jig head, (4) airplane jig, (5) ¾-ounce Northland Sting'r Bucktail, (6) ½-ounce Ripple Tail.

Jigging for Winter Lakers

Jigging for lakers is not much different than jigging for walleyes. The gear you use is a little heavier, and the jigs are slightly larger, but the jigging technique is pretty much the same. Give the bait a slight twitch, pause several seconds until it settles to rest, then twitch again.

As in any other kind of jigging, there is no right or wrong action. Some days the fish want practically no movement; other days, they want 6-foot sweeps. You just have to experiment to see what's working. Whatever jigging motion you use, always pause long enough between strokes to let your jig settle to a complete rest; lakers will seldom strike the jig while it's moving. Here's a trick that will sometimes trigger a strike when nothing else is working: Jig your bait about a dozen times without pausing; then stop jigging and wait for 10 or 15 seconds. Repeat this process several times. It's sort of like teasing a cat with a piece of string.

The majority of the trout I catch in winter are within 5 feet of the bottom, but there are times when they're suspended as much as 30 feet off bottom. If you spot high-riding fish on your electronics, reel up so your jig is just above them. If they follow the jig as you move it up and down, they're probably trout.

Keeping your jig just above the fish is the key to successful jigging. Lakers seem to focus most of their attention on what's going on above them; if you jig at their level or below them, you're less likely to get hits. If you're not using electronics, do most of your jigging about 3 or 4 feet off bottom, reeling up occasionally to jig at about 10 or 20 feet above the bottom. Always gauge your depth by dropping the lure to the bottom and then counting the number of turns of the reel handle as you reel up. Let's say you're getting bites 7 turns off bottom; then you can easily return to the same depth.

When you hook a good-sized laker, play it carefully. It may come up easily at first, making you think that landing it will be a snap. Then, just as you're about to bring it into the hole, it gets new life and makes a screeching run for the bottom. If you don't believe this can happen, I'll show you the broken jigging rod I kept as a souvenir.

HOW TO TIP A JIG WITH CUT BAIT

Scale a good-size sucker or other fresh baitfish. Then, using a very sharp filet knife, cut off one filet.

Remove the bones that form the rib cage and trim away the thicker meat along the back so the overall thickness of the filet is fairly even.

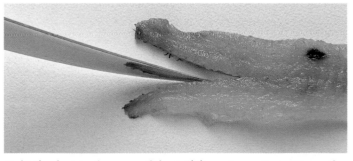

Split the last inch or so of the tail for extra action. Taper the front end of the filet so it is no more than ¼-inch wide at the tip.

Push the jig hook through the tip of the filet as shown. Insert the stinger hook just ahead of the split in the tail.

Winter lakers like some flash.

Jig-Fishing Tips

Splice a small barrel swivel into your leader about 2 feet above the jig. Otherwise, line twist will become a problem when you're jigging in deep water.

Slip a pre-tied stinger hook with a rubber-coated loop onto the bend of your jig hook. You can add this type of stinger in seconds and it won't come off.

Use a depth finder with a fold-up arm for hanging the transducer in the water. This way, when you move to a new hole, you don't have to readjust the transducer.

COPING WITH GREAT LAKES CURRENTS

by Tom Huggler

The average Great Lakes salmon troller has little understanding of one of the major factors affecting his fishing success: current. We're not talking river current, but current within the open waters of these huge lakes. Even on the most placid days, these unseen currents are present.

The current comes from many sources. The Great Lakes' 5,747 tributaries, ranging from mere trickles to raging torrents, are a major contributor. Powerful winds also push massive amounts of water, sometimes raising water levels on the downwind shore as much as 8 feet! Other current contributors, according to scientists, include condensation, evaporation, turnover and even moon-induced tides.

Nowhere are the effects of current more evident than in Lake Ontario. Although the smallest of the five Great Lakes in terms of surface area, Lake Ontario is the second-deepest lake after Superior. Although Ontario is only 193 miles long and 53 miles wide, its average depth is nearly 300 feet. The large volume of cold water offers outstanding salmon fishing while contributing to enormous temperature fluctuations which cause – and in turn are caused by – current. Because of the lake's east-to-west orientation, prevailing westerlies are allowed a clean sweep, but the biggest factor that contributes to current dynamics is the inflow from the Niagara River.

The mighty Niagara is more like a strait than a river. According to engineers at the New York Power Authority, which operates a dam on the river, the Niagara sends about 1.5 million gallons per second into the southwestern end of Lake Ontario. Besides pumping food into the lake, the Niagara's emerald-gray plume travels the lake's entire length, creating temperature and color breaks that influence zooplankton, baitfish, trout and salmon.

How powerful is this current? "Olcott, New York, lies 18 miles east of the river's outflow," says Bob Cinelli, one of Lake Ontario's most respected charter-boat captains. "A mile off shore from the harbor village is a 5-foot-high buoy. I have seen currents moving so fast through this area that they literally bury the buoy some distance underwater."

Cinelli, like most of the Great Lakes' best salmon trollers, understands current and knows how to fish it to his advantage. He knows, for example, where fish lie in relation to current and how current affects their feeding and migrational patterns. He also knows that current can make or break a salmon troller's game plan and that he must adjust his lure presentation to compensate for it.

"Probably 90 percent of the lake is unused by salmon and trout at any given time," Cinelli says. "Fish may travel through some of that large volume of water, but the truth is they hold and feed in only 10 percent of it. Those are the fish I look for, and current is the place I begin my homework."

How Current
Affects Your Fishing

Here are some examples of just how important current can be in planning your fishing strategy:

In spring, salmon and trout abound near the mouth of the Niagara River, because it is much warmer than the surrounding lake water and carries food. Shallow Lake Erie heats up faster than deeper Lake Ontario, and the Niagara River is the conduit for the warmer flow. A northwest wind loads Lake Ontario's southern shoreline with warm water, and trollers begin scoring all the way to Rochester. In summer, Cinelli avoids the Niagara River plume because it is typically too warm to attract fish.

Wind-generated currents also have a dramatic effect. In summer, Cinelli fishes the southeast shoreline of the lake. He favors south or southwest winds at that time, because they carry food and push the warm water away from shore, toward Canada. Cold water rolls up to replace it, drawing salmon closer to shore.

The Niagara River carries warm water from Lake Erie into Lake Ontario

Northwest winds are bad news because they push warm water into shore. During one recent summer when northerly winds prevailed, fishing was poor because the water was 72 degrees from the surface to 120 feet deep. The near-shore waters became a desert with fish abandoning the area for colder water. The next summer, however, southerly winds were the rule, and angling success improved dramatically.

Winds also create "slicks," which are localized current patterns that create a smooth area on the surface. "Sometimes you'll see a slick area next to choppy water," Cinelli says. "The water color may change and you may even notice trash lines developing. These are windrowed lines of leaves, duck weed and other debris, like bugs and pollen. Slicks draw baitfish and the trout and salmon follow."

Finding the elusive kings in summer can be tough. Cinelli relies heavily on his electronics to find the fish and compensate for the currents. "I need three numbers from my electronics to tell me how much current I am dealing with and which direction it is coming from," he says. "The first number is my surface speed, which I get from a surface-speed indicator that also measures temperature. The second is a speed reading that I get from an indicator on the downrigger weight. The third is a GPS reading that gives me speed over the lake bottom." The illustration on the opposite page explains how Cinelli uses these three numbers.

At first glance, it seems that the most important number would be the speed at the downrigger weight, because that's what determines the action of the spoons running at that level. But Cinelli often runs spoons near the surface and in the middle depths as well.

What really complicates matters is the fact that you're often dealing with shear currents. In other words, the current at the surface is moving the opposite direction as that in the depths. So it's possible that you could be trolling at the ideal speed for the spoons in deep water, but those in shallow water would virtually be standing still and have no action. If that's the case, your surface-speed indicator could be reading zero m.p.h. while your GPS is registering 2 or 3 m.p.h. Without these electronics you would have no idea of what is happening and you would be unable to find a trolling angle that would keep all your spoons running at an acceptable speed.

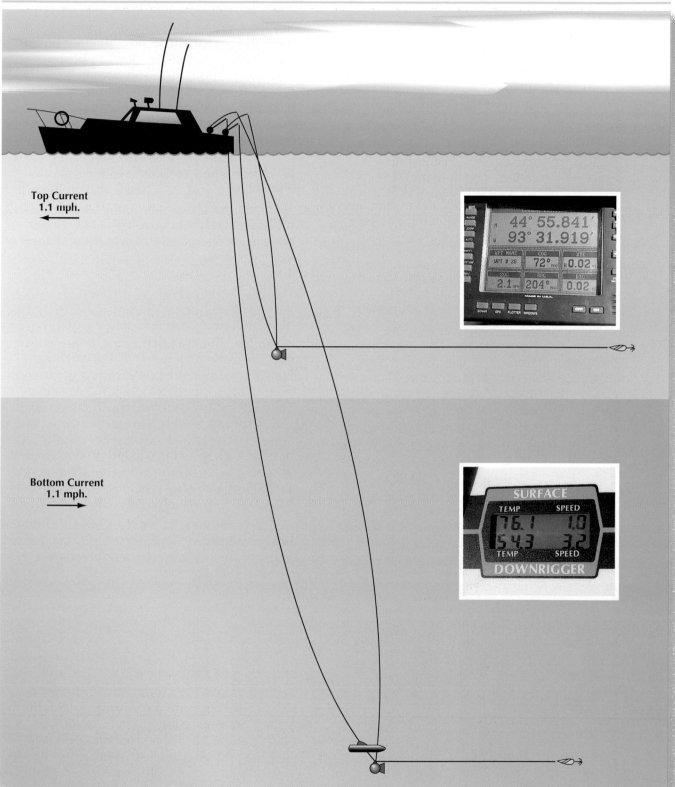

In this example, the GPS reading is 2.1 mph (top inset), the surface speed 1.0 mph (bottom inset, top right reading), and the speed at the downrigger weight, 3.2 mph (bottom inset, bottom right reading). That means you're trolling with a surface current of 1.1 mph, and against a current of 1.1 mph at the downrigger weight. Depending on which spoons you're using, the shallower spoons may not be running fast enough to have the right action, and the deeper spoons may be running too fast. To correct the problem, troll across the current rather than parallel to it. Keep adjusting your trolling angle until all spoons are running at the desired speed.

Trolling Strategies

"Trolling is by far the best method for Great Lakes salmon," Cinelli says, "because it allows you to cover the most water. You could catch salmon by drifting with bait or jigging, but you wouldn't be able to stay with the fish."

"The key is moving quickly from spot to spot. If I hear somebody on the radio catching fish 3 miles away, I have to make a decision. Do I want to pick up my lines and run, or do I want to troll over to them? If I'm trolling into a current, it would take too much time to get there. But if I'm going with the current, it won't take long."

"That's why I prefer trolling with the current. Of course, I cover more water that way as well, and that helps me find active fish."

"If the surface current is moving west to east, as it normally does in Lake Ontario, I'll run to the west and troll back with it. Or, if there is a shear current, I may troll across it. That way, I can keep all my spoons running at the right speed. Plus, when you troll perpendicular to the current, you're pulling the spoons across the fishes' faces, which is a good way to trigger strikes."

From the beginning of the season through August, Cinelli relies heavily on spoons. Most other fishermen mix spoons with plugs, and some run purely a plug program. There are times when Cinelli switches to a dodger-fly combination, but spoons account for 80 per-cent of the 1,500 trout and salmon brought aboard his boat in an average year.

Why spoons? "I'm certainly more confident using them," Cinelli admits, "but the truth is spoons give me a better hookup percentage. Because we troll, these fish have to hook themselves. Thin, flat spoons fit into their mouths better. The round shape of most plugs gives a fish more leverage to throw the hook." Cinelli is also a fanatic about sharp hooks. He files his hooks to pinprick sharpness and screws down his releases to maximize his hooking percentage.

Cinelli has more than 5,000 spoons aboard his charter boat, but he relies mainly on six types (opposite page) to cover the spectrum of trolling speeds, from .5 to 5 mph, and to fish effectively in different currents.

Shape and thickness of a spoon determine the speed at which it performs best. As a rule, the bigger the bend, the slower a spoon must be trolled. The thicker the metal, the faster it must be trolled. Honey Bee and Michigan Stinger spoons work best at very slow speeds, from .5 to 1.5 mph, although the Michigan Stinger can also be fished much faster. These spoons produce when fish are lethargic and currents are minimal. Optimizer spoons are best for high-speed trolling, with good action at speeds up to 5 mph or even a little faster. Yeck, Northern King and Pro King spoons all work well at medium to medium-fast speeds.

Colors are important to Cinelli's success. The hot color in early morning is typically char-treuse; however, as the day brightens, he

HOW TO STACK SPOONS ON DOWNRIGGERS

Let out about 10 feet of line and attach it to the downrigger release. Lower the ball 5 feet or more, depending on the desired stacking distance. Place the rod in a rod holder with the clicker on.

Let out about 10 feet of line on the second rod and attach it to a stacker on the downrigger cable. Place the rod in a rod holder with the clicker on. If desired, add a second stacker.

Lower the downrigger to the desired depth and then take up the slack in both lines until the rods bow over. When a fish strikes, the rod will stand up straight.

mixes in black, then switches over to pink by afternoon. As the sun works its way toward the western horizon, he gradually merges in blacks again. By nightfall, his spread is solid black.

Cinelli buys mostly blank spoons and then doctors them with tape patterns. He likens the process to a stream trout fisherman who enjoys tying his own flies. "Some store-bought patterns work well," he says, "but I have better success when I make little changes such as widening or narrowing stripes and adding eyes."

Cinelli's reels are spooled with clear, 20-pound-test premium monofilament, but he admits that he uses stronger-than-needed line to help "customer-proof" his tackle from anglers who don't know how to handle salmon. In the hands of an experienced fisherman, 10- to 14-pound-test monofilament is sufficient.

Cinelli watches the little things, too. For example, the size of baitfish that salmon and trout are eating is important, as well as how they are taking lures. Aggressive fish usually are hooked in the corner of the mouth; finicky biters, in the upper jaw. Switching lures or making presentations at different angles into the current can turn fussy eaters into voracious ones.

"You have to remember that these fish are high-energy eating machines," Cinelli says. "When a salmon wants your lure, he'll come after it like a mad dog. My job is to make him take the lure."

CINELLI'S FAVORITE SALMON SPOONS

(1) Honey Bee , (2) Pro King, (3) Northern King, (4) Michigan Stinger, (5) Optimizer, (6) Yeck Spoon.

Cinelli mounts all four of his downriggers close to the boat corners. He believes the "corner out-downs" outproduce all other locations. He usually stacks similar lures that run well at the same speed 5 and 10 feet above the outdowns (opposite). On the two inside downriggers, he stacks spoons to run a little shallower. This gives him an inverted "V" pattern. The leads (amount of line behind the downriggers) are all short, about 5 to 10 feet, for better hooksetting. The short leads, along with the V pattern, help keep the lures from tangling.

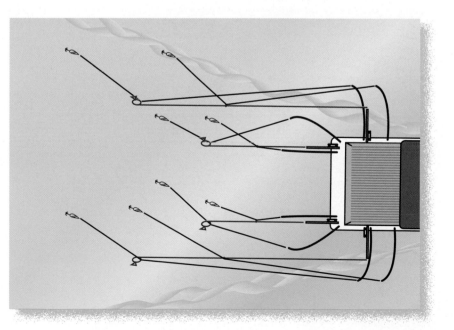

THE DROP-BACK TECHNIQUE FOR RIVER STEELHEAD

By Dave Richey

Lake Michigan is blessed with some of the country's best steelhead rivers, a fact of which Emil Dean of Bear Lake, Michigan, is well aware. But the sleek, silvery fighters have a distinct stubborn streak and are difficult to extract from any stream, let alone the big, wide, fast-moving rivers along the Michigan shoreline of this huge fish pond. Dean – who is often called the "Dean of Charterboat Skippers"– has devised and perfected a unique method for consistently taking steelhead in these waters.

The reason steelhead in the rivers are so hard to catch is that they're entering the rivers to spawn, not feed. They will not go out of their way to chase a bait, so you must put it right in their faces. Using what he calls the "drop-back technique," Dean does exactly that. He anchors directly upstream from a run that is likely to hold steelhead and then lets the current carry a crankbait down to them, keeping enough tension on the bait so that it wiggles enticingly right in front of their noses.

The Steelhead Spawning Cycle

"Steelhead move upstream from Lake Michigan in fall, winter and spring," Dean explains. "Fall and winter fish spend all winter in the stream, and spawn in late March or April. When fall steelies winter over in the stream they become darker in color than their fresh-run, silvery cousins that move up in the spring."

As spawning time nears, their appearance begins to change. Males develop a broad red band along the lateral line, brilliant red or orange-red gill covers and cheeks, and an enormous, hooked lower jaw, or kype, which is common in some other spawning trout and salmon.

Males move in first; females, or hens, usually arrive just before spawning time. They are fresh from Lake Michigan and cloaked in a coat of silvery scales as bright as a newly minted dime. The courtship is brief, and once spawning begins on shallow gravel bars, a hen will lay her eggs in one or two days while attended by two to six males.

Steelhead do not all mature at the same time. "The trout often begin their pre-spawn staging routine off the river mouth," Dean notes, "and then trickle upstream a few fish at a time. They don't run all at once, and that's why

Steelhead dig redds in gravel like this.

Male steelhead have bright red gill covers and cheeks.

Hen steelhead are more silvery than the males and have a shorter head.

fishing can be good over a period of several weeks during the fall, winter and spring periods."

Often, large numbers of fish move upstream following heavy runoff that increases the river's flow.

Rising water from the spring thaw draws steelhead into spawning streams.

Best Conditions for Steelheading

Rising water not only draws more fish into a stream, the current surge washes in food and seems to trigger steelies into striking. A rise may be caused by increasing runoff or, if the river is controlled by a dam, more water being released. But fishing can also be good when the water is receding. Dean believes that fishing is generally better when the water level is changing than when it's stable.

"They often open a dam for a few hours and then close it again," Dean explains. "The water starts to rise, reaches its peak and begins falling again, all within a two- or three-hour period. That's when the fish usually bite."

Another good time for steelhead is the clear-out after a period of gloomy weather. "If it's cloudy, cold, raining or snowing, and the sun suddenly peeks out, the fish turn on," Dean says. "That's the best time of all to catch steelhead."

"I've seen it happen hundreds of times through the years. The sun comes out for a few minutes and the fish go nuts. I tell my clients to fish hard whenever the sun is out."

Long runs with slow- to moderate-speed current make excellent steelhead spots. The best runs have a fairly slick surface and good-sized rocks or boulders to serve as current breaks.

Tail-outs of pools hold steelhead that are resting up after struggling through the downstream rapids.

Current seams form at the junction of slow and fast water. Steelhead hold right along the seam (dotted line).

Deep pools that form below rapids may hold large numbers of steelhead. The fish hold in the slow-moving water until another runoff surge draws them farther upstream.

The Drop-Back Technique

Dean believes ripening males and females will hold in runs, deep pools and other pockets of relatively quiet water near any obstruction that breaks the current. He pointed out one such spot as we motored upstream under the jet power in his customized, heated riverboat. He nosed the bow of his boat into a log jam 25 yards above a slick run that paralleled the riverbank. The run was about 100 yards long, 10 yards wide and 12 feet deep.

"This looks good," Dean said, as the boat nosed up to the jumble of logs. He hit a switch and 50-pounds of heavy chain eased to the bottom from his bow-mounted anchor winch. "It takes 50 pounds of weight on heavy anchor-cable to hold the boat in the proper position to fish this run."

When fishing slow current with the drop-back technique, Dean prefers a FlatFish. When the water is deeper and faster, he uses Tadpollys, Wiggle Warts, Wee Warts, Wee Steelie Warts or Hot 'N Tots. His favorite colors are silver or chrome-plate, yellow with black stripes and gray-pearl. He also likes red-and-white, as well as gold.

Steelhead may hold anywhere in a slick run like the one we were fishing. Runs up to 75 yards in length can be fished from one anchor

position. Longer runs mean picking up the anchor, drifting downstream and anchoring again to fish the bottom half of the run.

He rigged three outfits consisting of an 8-foot, light-power, slow-action baitcasting rod and an Ambassadeur 5000 baitcasting reel spooled with 20-pound FireLine and an 8-foot leader of clear, 12-pound mono. He attached the lure with a small Cross-Loc snap.

The technique is fairly simple and can be learned in just a few minutes. Hold the rod in your left hand with the reel in free-spool. While thumbing the reel, let out about 25 feet of line. Let the lure wiggle in the current for about 30 seconds (longer during very cold weather), and then ease off the thumb pressure to let out another three feet of line. Hold it for another 30 seconds, let out three feet more, and repeat until you've covered the entire run.

I had just dropped back three feet when a lightning jolt shot up my arm and the rod tip slammed down to the water. The steelie instantly rocketed to the surface and twisted head-over-tail across the water. "It's a bright fish," Dean said. "Looks like a fresh hen – about 12 pounds. Just keep light pressure on her and I'll clear the other lines."

The fish bored across the river current, twisted into the air again, made a belly-flop, and then sounded for bottom. Dean raised the anchor chain and we slowly began drifting downstream toward the fish as it wallowed on the surface. After five minutes of bulldog runs,

DROPPING BACK FOR STEELHEAD

Anchor at the head of a long run or pool, where the current speed is slow enough to hold steelhead.

With your reel in free-spool, let out about 25 feet of line and let your lure hang in the current. Thumb the spool while the lure wiggles in the current.

(1) Tadpolly, (2) &(4) Wee Warts, (3) Hot 'N Tot, (5) FlatFish, (6) Wiggle Wart.

Dean slid the mesh of his big landing net under the exhausted fish. We took a few quick pictures, he lowered the hen steelie over the side and she immediately darted out of sight.

The majority of the holes and runs that Dean fishes can be covered in one drop, but some, like the 100-yard-long run we were fishing, require two. After a few more drops through the upper end, we raised the anchor, slipped down to the middle of the run and anchored again to work the bottom end of the run.

We ended a perfect day with a double header, including a bright 15-pound hen.

Dean's drop-back technique is ideal for inexperienced anglers because they don't have to worry about detecting subtle strikes. There's no doubt when a steelhead hits the lure; it's a wrist-spraining jolt that will jerk the rod out of the hands of an unsuspecting angler.

The drop-back method works well in any river large enough to accommodate a boat. It doesn't always produce large numbers of fish, but it accounts for some of the biggest steelhead taken each year. And judging from my experience, it's the most exciting brand of steelhead action developed in years.

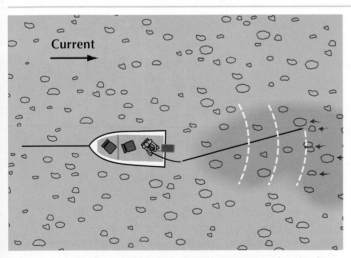

Let out line 3 feet at a time, pausing to let the lure wiggle for about 30 seconds after each drop.

Lift anchor to go after a big fish, rather than try to reel it back through the run. This way, you're less likely to spook other fish that may be holding in the run.

Pike & Muskie

Removing the mystery from America's most misunderstood gamefish.

DEAD BAIT FOR WINTERTIME PIKE

by Dick Sternberg

Few fish are as aggressive in frigid water as northern pike. They spend a good deal of their time cruising about in search of food, especially during the first few weeks of the ice-cover season. Their activity slows a little in midwinter, but picks up again in the weeks before ice-out. Muskies, on the other hand, feed only sporadically in winter and and are rarely taken by ice anglers.

In lakes where low oxygen levels slow the activity of most other gamefish, pike continue to move about and feed. They can tolerate surprisingly low oxygen levels and are one of the last species to die when a lake freezes out.

You may take an occasional pike by jigging, but you'll normally do better by setting out a tip-up and a good-sized baitfish. Wintertime pike are lazy; they'd rather cruise about until they find one big meal than chase down a dozen small ones. Traditionally, pike anglers have baited their tip-ups with a lively sucker, chub or shiner from 5 to 7 inches long. But savvy fishermen have discovered that pike often seem more interested in dead baitfish, particularly oily, smelly ones like smelt or cisco. Why does dead bait work so well? Not only are pike known scent feeders, it takes practically no energy to swim up and inhale dead bait.

The best way to rig dead bait on a tip-up is to use a quick-strike rig made with a pair of double or treble hooks. You push one hook into the baitfish near the pectoral fin; the other, just in front of the dorsal fin. This way, you can set the hook immediately when a pike strikes. Not only will you hook more of the fish that strike, you have a better chance of successfully releasing fish you don't want, because you don't give them a chance to swallow the hook.

You can easily make a quick-strike rig using 30-pound-test wire leader material and a pair of size 2 to 4 treble hooks. Or you can buy ready-made rigs from several sources. My favorite is the Quickset Rig (below), which has supersharp double hooks with the back hook rigged to slide. This way, you can adjust the spacing between the hooks to fit any baitfish.

Another way to rig dead baitfish is to hang them on a Swedish hook (bottom).

To rig a dead baitfish on a Quickset Rig, push the smaller hook of the front double hook into the body near the pectoral fin, then push the small hook of the rear double hook into the back, just ahead of the dorsal fin.

To rig the bait on a Swedish hook, hold the hook shank down and push it into the bait's vent as far as the hook bend. Then, turn the hook shank up and push the point through the back so it comes out just behind the head.

Tip-Up Fishing

Tips-ups enable you to cover a large area, increasing your chances of finding pike. Most states allow you to use at least two lines for ice fishing, so if there are several anglers in your party, you can scatter tip-ups over a good-sized bay or cover a long section of a breakline.

It pays to buy quality tip-ups. One of the most popular is the Polar Tip-up, which has an unbreakable plastic frame that will last indefinitely. The exposed T-bar spins when the spool turns, so you can easily read the fish's movements.

Go with braided Dacron or nylon-coated tip-up line, which won't soak up water and freeze. Use line from 25- to 40-pound test, and add a 20- to 30-pound-test braided-wire leader.

Start by setting the bait 6 to 12 inches above the bottom. If that doesn't work, experiment with different depth settings. Sometimes pike will pick up dead bait right off the bottom; other times they prefer bait hung only a foot under the ice. When the flag pops up, grab the line and set the hook firmly.

The excitement of tip-up fishing quickly gets in your blood. You spot a flag, sprint over to the hole and see the T-bar whirling. Then, you set the hook and the line smokes through your fingers. To a die-hard ice-fisherman, that's heaven.

A spindle-type tip-up has (1) a frame that stretches across the hole, (2) an underwater reel, (3) a spindle that turns when the reel turns, releasing the (4) spring-loaded flag.

How to Use a Tip-Up

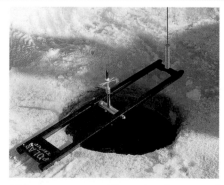

Drop your bait to the desired depth, then set the flag arm under the spindle, as shown. Setting the arm under the grooved end of the spindle makes the tip-up harder to trip.

When you see a flag, check to see if the spindle is turning. If it is, set the hook. If it's not, gently pull on the line until you feel the weight of the fish, and then set the hook.

Snap your wrist sharply to set the hook but be ready to feed line when the fish runs. When you retrieve line, stack it neatly. This way, it won't tangle should the fish make another run.

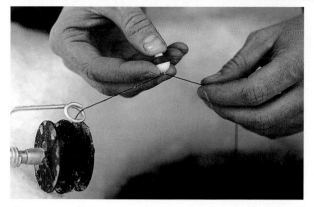

Once you determine the right depth, pinch a small split shot onto your line just below the reel. Or, clip on a tiny bobber. This way, you can easily reset your line without having to measure the depth again.

Use a wind tip-up to give the bait a little movement. Wind blowing on the metal plate makes the arm bob up and down. In very cold weather, however, wind tip-ups are prone to freeze-up because the spool is above water.

Store your tip-up with the wire leader stretched out to prevent kinking. Wrap a heavy rubber band around the tip-up frame, loop the line around the reel handle (inset) and attach the hook to the rubber band as shown.

Land big pike with a gaff, but only if you plan to keep them. A heavy pike is difficult to pull up through a hole with the line, especially when the ice is thick.

Taper the bottom of your hole with an ice chisel. It's hard to get a big pike started up the hole. But with the bottom tapered, they'll slide through much more easily.

MUSKIES AFTER DARK

by Dean Bortz

Only a decade ago, most fishermen assumed muskies were pretty much like northern pike. After the sun went down, fishing for them was a waste of time. But a small fraternity of anglers discovered that muskies go on the prowl under the cover of darkness, and their night fishing techniques are no longer the well-kept secret that they once were.

The majority of muskie hunters believe that these fish sulk their way through the long hot summers and are extremely difficult to catch. But with the discovery of night fishing, even veteran anglers in the muskie country of northern Wisconsin have revised their thinking.

If anyone is creating a bulge on the night fishing learning curve, it has to be Joe Bucher of Eagle River, Wisconsin. Anyone talking to Bucher for a few minutes will be convinced there is no better way to approach summer muskies than under a cloak of darkness.

Considering his muskie fishing success in recent years, there is no reason to doubt him. In one three-night stand, he and his clients caught 28 legal muskies, including a 50-incher. The catch was no fluke. A few weeks earlier, he and some other clients caught 29. The high point of the week came one night when an angler who had never caught a legal muskie in 35 years of fishing landed six of them.

Bucher, a northern Wisconsin fishing guide, lure manufacturer, writer and fishing educator, discovered the benefits of night fishing during the early 1970s – even before he began guiding.

At that time, he played lead guitar and sang in a Milwaukee band. His gigs lasted until 2 or 3 a.m., then he headed home to get in a few hours of walleye or bass fishing before turning in.

"The lake was full of water skiers during the day," Bucher recalls. "By the time I finished playing, the boats had been off the water for about five hours and the fish were active. They had adapted to the pressure. It seemed like most of the gamefish, except pike, fed after dark because of the traffic."

That knowledge became useful once Bucher began guiding for muskies in the mid-1970s. At that time, most northern Wisconsin guides picked up their clients at 8 a.m. and dropped them off at 4 p.m. Fishing wasn't bad in spring and early summer, but once the dog days hit, the action stopped. Good guides brought in maybe one muskie every three days.

Bucher didn't like the results and, because he began getting into the tackle business about the same time, he switched his guiding to morning and evening outings.

"The mornings were okay, but the evenings were definitely better. Most anglers at that time did not believe muskies fed after dark. If they caught one, they thought it was just getting in a late feed," he says.

As Bucher stayed on the water later and later, it soon became obvious that he was catching more and bigger fish at twilight. His afternoon outings ran from 2 p.m. until dark for three years and, as time progressed, "dark" kept getting later and later. He started noticing that the first seven hours, from 2 to 9 p.m., wasn't as hot as the one hour after 9. Checking back through his logs, it didn't take him long to figure out that more than 70 percent of his muskies came after sunset.

Then, in 1983, Bucher diverged from the norm even more, guiding clients from 5 p.m. to midnight. His success rate skyrocketed!

"That was my greatest year of muskie fishing – we averaged two to three muskies a night and there were times when we boated eight or nine," Bucher says. "It changed everything."

Not only do muskies feed at night because of heavy daytime boat traffic, but also because they have good night vision. If they couldn't see well, they would be forced to feed during the day, regardless of traffic.

"The biggest difference between a muskie and a northern pike is vision," Bucher says. "Pike simply have poorer eyesight and that may be why they're easier to catch. Fishermen can trigger pike into striking and I have noticed that where the both species are present, pike will be caught in the clearer water.

"That difference may explain why pike aren't often caught at night and why muskies tend to follow; they see leaders. It may also explain why so many big muskies are caught by unsuspecting anglers using light line; it's less visible."

Muskies also seem less wary and more aggressive after dark. The cover of darkness camouflages leaders, lines, boats and angler movement.

During his early days of night guiding, Bucher fished mainly on the surface, using wooden topwaters. "I'd drive to the landing," he recalls, "and if it was windy, I wouldn't go out. I didn't realize that I was missing the best action – fishing wind-blown water with sub-surface lures." Bucher believes that the wind makes muskies less spooky. Instead of finding one fish on a spot, he frequently finds several.

Bucktail spinners accounted for quite a few subsurface muskies, but Bucher suspected that the fish were having trouble detecting them in choppy water. So he began experimenting, using larger baits and adding bigger blades to produce more vibration.

That change soon began to pay big dividends. On one hot, humid night with a southwest wind, Bucher and his party took eight muskies, with seven coming from the same bar. Bucher knew he was onto something and, as he learned more, the word began to spread.

Besides the boat-traffic issue, some fishermen believe that night fishing is effective because they are working an entirely "untouched" group of fish. Avid night anglers have noticed that many muskies caught after dark are "clean," meaning they have not been hooked, netted and released by other fishermen. Their mouths and fins are not torn, their scales are not scraped. Telemetry research with other species, such as walleyes, has uncovered the existence of sub-populations of fish of the same species, in the same body of water. These groups of fish display behavior patterns that vary from those of other fish. They occupy different habitats and use different spawning areas. Night fishermen believe the same is true with muskies.

When & Where to Night Fish

Bucher begins fishing different lakes at different times of the year, with the amount of boat traffic being the primary determinant of the day to night change. Boat traffic begins early on popular waters, such as Vilas County's Eagle chain or Oneida County's Minocqua chain, so that's the time to begin night fishing.

In most cases, however, night fishing turns on around the end of June and continues through July and August and into mid-September. After September, night fishing becomes iffy. The fall night-bite resembles a cold-front bite in many respects. Of course, cold fronts occur frequently late in the year.

Bucher once caught a 28-pound muskie after dark on November 6, when the water temperature was 43 degrees. He was slow-trolling near a school of ciscoes at the time and that may be the key to catching late-season muskies in cisco lakes. The silvery members of the whitefish family spawn in shallow water after dark in November.

Certain physical characteristics can make one lake better than another for night fishing. A good night fishing lake should have an abundance of shallow, weedy cover to serve as a feeding area. In contrast, deep lakes with sparse weeds often make better trolling lakes than night fishing lakes, especially if the lack of cover is coupled with good oxygen levels at all depths. Even if such a lake has heavy boat traffic, fish will continue to feed during the day in deep water.

Night fishermen should also consider water clarity. Fish will be active at night in stained or clear water, but they'll be shallower in the stained water.

Of course, it helps to select a lake with a good muskie population. Make a choice, get to know the lake and fish it under all weather conditions, including cold fronts. In fact, the night following a cold front may be the best time to catch a muskie.

Bucher has discovered that muskies stick their noses in the weeds and rarely feed on "bluebird days" with mile-high skies after a cold front.

On the night following a front, however, they often feed in a short burst of activity right after dusk.

That feeding spree relates directly to the fading light. As shadows fall across weed edges and rock bars, the fish become active. Knowing there is only a short time to capitalize on the cold-front behavior, anglers familiar with the lake's feeding areas plan a precise route, hoping to encounter fish as they begin to turn on.

Since shadows first cover a lake's west side, the western weed edges are the first places to hit. Similar shadows fall on the east side of points and islands. Muskies on rock bars will normally feed later than "weed fish" in the same area, perhaps because the rock bars lack cover and the muskies aren't comfortable in open areas until it gets darker.

The biggest secret to night fishing success is learning a lake well enough to predict feeding times. On one lake, Bucher discovered a weed ledge on the lake's west end that turned on regularly at 8:45 p.m. Another spot, a rock bar out in the lake, did not turn on until 10:10 p.m. during July. In both cases, fish activity was triggered by changing light conditions.

Deep running crankbaits are useful on cold front nights. The fish feed in the same spots that are used during more active periods, but they stick closer to the bottom.

"During an active period, fishermen can be successful using surface baits or bucktails above weeds, but I found that, during cold fronts, deep-diving crankbaits caught more and bigger fish because the bait gets down to where the fish are," Bucher says.

PEAK MUSKIE-FISHING TIMES

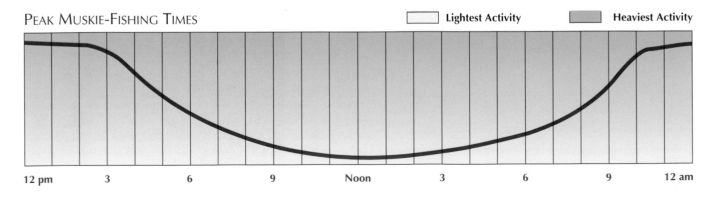

| | Lightest Activity | | Heaviest Activity |

12 pm   3   6   9   Noon   3   6   9   12 am

As darkness sets in, concentrate on shadowed areas (western side) of the lake first, because that's where the fish first start to feed.

How to Pick a Night Fishing Lake

Look for lakes with a shallow food shelf and plenty of submerged vegetation, such as cabbage weed, for cover. Muskies move up on the shelf to feed at dusk.

In deep lakes with no food shelf, muskies cruise the depths and feed throughout the day, so night fishing is not as effective.

(1) M/G Sunset Spinnerbait,
(2) Buchertail spinner, (3) Tallywacker,
(4) Depth Raider.

Night Fishing Equipment and Techniques

A good depth finder is a must for finding weed edges in the dark. LCRs, however, are next to useless unless they are backlit. Flashers just may be the night fisherman's best friend. The bright flashing light tells a night owl everything he needs to know.

Headlamps are the night angler's next most valuable piece of equipment. Unlike flashlights, headlamps are rarely misplaced, can be turned on quickly once a fish is hooked and seldom fall in the lake.

Bucher uses 7-to 7½-foot, heavy-power rods and baitcasting reels smaller than normal muskie reels. "The smaller reels have internal parts identical to the larger reels," he says, "but they are easier to hold on to. The only difference is line capacity, but you're making shorter casts at night."

If baits don't have hooks on split rings, they do after Bucher gets through modifying them. Then, muskies cannot "torque" against the bait, so fewer fish get away. Of course, all hooks should be well sharpened.

The boat should be clear of all gear other than what's being used at the time. Nets or gaffs should be handy, but out of the way. Leave the front running lights on while fishing and carry a spotlight that can be used to scan the lake while motoring.

You can use any of four bait types for night fishing: winged surface baits, spinnerbaits, bucktails or crankbaits.

Surface baits are retrieved very slowly above the weeds. The plopping noise, wake and silhouette give muskies something to aim at.

When using topwaters, wait until you feel the fish's weight before setting the hook. Muskies have a habit of surfacing behind a bait and tracking it for several feet before striking. That can unnerve a fishermen in the dark, causing an early hookset and sending the bait right back at the angler's face. To avoid that, set the hooks by sweeping the rod down and to the side.

Spinnerbaits and bucktails can be used between the surface and weed tops. When using spinnerbaits, Bucher prefers single blades that are flattened with a hammer. Flat blades create more vibration. Spinnerbaits are also useful because the blade helicopters when dropped into weed pockets. Bucktails should be oversized with large blades. Both bucktails and spinnerbaits can be worked along weed edges, but no bait is as effective along the weed edges as a crankbait.

Bucher uses crankbaits more often now that he has perfected the Depth Raider, a jointed crankbait made from the same plastic that is used to make bulletproof car windows. He developed the Depth Raider after years of using wooden crankbaits. A plastic bait is more durable than wood, and allows for a better hookset because the fish can't sink their teeth into it.

The lure also makes a clacking noise when the jointed segments hit together during the retrieve. Bucher still has the original prototype; although he has caught more than 100 muskies on it, the bait is barely scratched. The bait runs at 10 feet when you're casting with 20-pound line; double that when you're trolling.

Deep-running crankbaits work better than surface baits or bucktails on cold-front nights. The fish feed on the same spots they did in more active periods, but they stick closer to the bottom.

Boat control is just as important as proper bait selection. Knowing one lake well not only allows fishermen to find active fish, it helps them stay on the weed edges. Following an edge is difficult enough during the day, and it's much tougher at night.

"Fishermen must know the lake intimately to effectively fish at night. They must also have sound techniques. A 'bad' crankbait fishermen during the day will be real bad at night. The same goes for boat control. Fishermen have to have good boat control during the day, but they need great boat control at night."

"It takes precise movement along a weed edge to be successful. The better you are at fundamentals, like casting, retrieving and boat control, the more fish you will catch," Bucher says.

There's nothing quite like chasing muskies under the stars. About the time you're trying to figure out which way the big dipper is pointing, a big muskie slashes your bait at boatside, stopping your heart for a second or two. You don't know when the fish are going to strike, because you can't see the follows – and that's what makes night fishing so exciting.

NIGHT FISHING TIPS

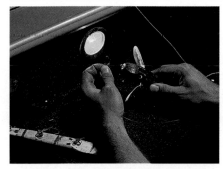

An interior boat light is a big help in rigging baits and unhooking fish.

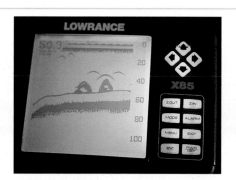

Select a depth finder that you can easily read after dark.

A headlamp works well for spotting boatside follows.

Split rings keep the hooks from binding, so the fish cannot dislodge them as easily.

Flatten spinnerbait blades to create extra vibration.

Leather gloves enable you to handle the fish without risk of injury.

SUMMERTIME PIKE: THE COLDWATER CONNECTION

by Dick Sternberg

When I was a kid, my dad sometimes took me fishing along the banks of Lake Pepin, a widening of the Mississippi River where it forms the Minnesota-Wisconsin boundary. We parked where a small creek flows into the lake and fished off the rocks. I liked that spot because I'd caught a couple of big pike there, one of which weighed a good 17 pounds.

I didn't realize what made that spot so productive until nearly two decades later. At that time, I was working on the Mississippi as a fisheries biologist for the Minnesota DNR and doing a lot of fishing. I began to discover certain spots that routinely produced big pike during the hottest part of the summer. I was not sure what drew the pike to these locations, and I didn't find out until I went back to fish them in the winter. Ice fishing was impossible in one spot, because the water was wide open and, in the others, there were small areas of open water along the shoreline. I then realized that every one of these spots was fed by a spring.

My fish sampling work confirmed what my sportfishing experience was telling me. Using electrofishing gear, I found huge pike holding in spots where you would never dream of fishing for them. I remember shocking four pike between 15 and 20 pounds off a 2-foot deep sandbar at the mouth of a small trout stream. The temperature where the stream entered the lake was 60°F, while the surrounding water was 78°F. I also found big pike in boat harbors where dredging had exposed springs on the bottom, in spots where runoff from ponds fed by artesian wells flowed into the lake, and around the mouths of coulee streams, spring-fed trickles that flowed into the river out of the surrounding hills. In some cases, the water temperature in these spring holes was as low as 48°F, the same temperature as ground water in that part of the country.

Since those early discoveries, I've continued to study the coldwater connection and have put together a pattern that helps me find and catch trophy pike during the heat of summer, when many anglers contend that the fish quit biting because they lose their teeth. The pattern applies everywhere pike are found, but it is much stronger in some situations than in others. The pattern is based on the following principles:

•Big pike (7 pounds or more) are strongly drawn to colder water whenever the water they normally inhabit exceeds 70°F. The more the temperature rises above 70, the stronger the draw of cold water becomes.

•Water only 2 or 3 degrees cooler will concentrate pike, but I prefer a differential of at least 10 degrees. I've found dense concentrations of pike in pockets of water as much as 35 degrees colder.

•Big pike are drawn to cold water much more strongly than smaller pike. Most gamefish prefer cooler water as they get larger, but this tendency is strongest in pike.

• Muskies do not exhibit the same coldwater habits as pike. I've taken an occasional muskie around a spring hole, but given a choice, they seem much more inclined to stay in warm water.

•Any type of cool water with adequate oxygen (more than 3 parts per million) will draw pike. Underwater springs and tributary streams provide cold water in many rivers and

some lakes. In lakes that form a thermocline with cool, well-oxygenated water beneath it, pike can retreat to deeper water when the shallows get too warm.

•Pike are easiest to locate around point sources of cold water, such as a spring or tributary, especially if it flows into a boat harbor, canal, small bay or other confined area where the cold water can collect. If a spring or tributary flows directly into a moving river or an open area of a lake, the current or wind will quickly dissipate the cold water.

•Productive pockets fed by point sources can be as shallow as 2 feet, but the best ones are within a long cast of water at least 7 feet deep. The best pockets I've found range from 5 to 15 feet in depth. One angler, however, wrote to tell me he regularly caught big pike around a spring hole in a Wisconsin lake, at a depth of 75 feet.

•Hot, calm weather is best. Intense heat drives pike into the cold water and, because there is no wind to dissipate the cold water, they stay there.

•Low water is more attractive than high water, especially in river fishing. Increased flows not only scatter the pike, they dilute the cold water more than normal and reduce the temperature difference.

•Because cold water is heavier than warm water, the prime fishing zone is usually near the bottom, assuming the oxygen content there is adequate. In the case of a small spring, the coldwater layer may be less than a foot thick, and that's where all the pike will be.

•Pike are lethargic in the cold water, and they're reluctant to leave it to chase food. This means you must virtually put the bait right in their face.

•When pike are removed from a coldwater pocket, more soon move in, usually within a couple days. Therefore, a good pocket can provide a seemingly endless supply of pike despite heavy fishing pressure.

Even if you're not aware of any springs or cold streams flowing into the waters you fish, it's important to understand the coldwater connection. First, there probably are coldwater pockets in some of the waters you fish, you just don't know about them. Second, understanding these principles will help you take more big pike in any body of water, even if these pockets don't exist.

Spring seeps are easy to find in winter – just look for steam and concentrations of waterfowl.

Where to Find Coldwater Pike

The easiest way to find point-source pockets is to scout for them in winter. Spring water stays at approximately the same temperature year-round, so it's cooler than the surrounding water in summer, but warmer in winter. And being warmer, it rises to the surface and prevents small, shallow-water areas of a lake or river from freezing. You'll often see waterfowl in the open holes and lots of steam rising up.

One die-hard pike hound reportedly chartered a small plane in winter so he could fly around and mark open-water pockets on his map. When you find such an ice-free pocket, come back and check the temperature the following summer. You'll need an electric thermometer with a cord long enough to reach bottom so you can pinpoint the coldwater zone.

Deep-water springs are much tougher to find. They don't show up in winter, because the water cools before it can reach the surface. Unless you're willing to spend days dragging an electric thermometer around the lake, you'll probably stumble on them only by accident. If you catch a couple big pike in a particular area, however, note the location carefully and check for cold water; you may have discovered a deep-water spring. Most good trout streams are spring-fed, and where these streams flow into warm-water lakes or rivers are natural places to start looking for big pike. Many states publish trout-stream guides that will help you pinpoint any such streams flowing into pike waters you fish.

But it doesn't take a big coldwater stream to draw pike; any spring-fed trickle has potential. One of my best pike holes is fed by two tiny springs that flow out of a hill, down a sandy beach and into the water. If you weren't paying attention, you wouldn't even see them. Don't expect to get much information on coldwater pockets by asking at the local bait shop – if anybody has discovered them, you can bet they're closely guarded secrets. You'll have to sleuth them out for yourself and fish them when conditions are right. But it's well worth the trouble, because once you find such a spot, it will yield big pike year after year.

Even if you're unable to find point-source pockets, coldwater pike principles still apply. In spring, anglers commonly catch good-sized pike in shallow, weedy bays of natural lakes. But the fish mysteriously disappear in summer, explaining the once widely-held belief that they quit biting because they've lost their teeth. True, pike continually shed their teeth and grow new ones, but no more in summer than at any other time. Poor summertime success usually results from fishing too shallow after warm weather has driven big pike to deeper, cooler water, leaving only the hammer-handles.

COMMON COLDWATER SOURCES

Trout streams and other small coldwater streams flowing into a warmwater river or lake draw pike.

Underwater springs that well up from the bottom of a bay or other protected area are pike magnets.

Seepage from shoreline springs may collect in deep holes near shore, attracting any big pike in the area.

TIPS FOR FINDING COLDWATER PIKE

An electric thermometer is a must for finding spring holes. It enables you to find the boundaries and thickness of the coldwater zone.

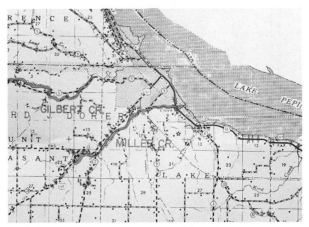

Trout stream maps show you where the streams flow into warmwater rivers or lakes, providing clues as to where big pike may be found.

Boat harbors, especially those that have been dredged, often produce giant pike. Dredging may expose springs, and the cold water can collect because the area is sheltered.

Shallow spring holes are formed by springs trickling in from shore.

Deep spring holes result from underwater springs flowing in from the bottom, forming a distinct cold-water layer.

How to Fish Coldwater Pockets

Precision is the key to catching pike around point-source coldwater pockets. In these pockets, which are often very small, the fish lie in a very narrow layer and are seldom in a chasing mood. The best way to draw their attention is to put a live bait right in their face by dangling it from a float (opposite).

A medium-heavy-power flippin' stick and a sturdy baitcasting reel spooled with 20-pound mono makes an ideal float-fishing setup. Dacron is not a good choice; it soaks up too much water and sinks, making it difficult to reel up slack and set the hook. The new superlines may have potential, assuming the brand you're using floats. Be sure your reel has a smooth drag; with mono, it should be tightened nearly to the line's breaking point to get a solid hookset. With superlines, I'd recommend loosening the drag a little more to lessen the shock factor.

There's nothing complicated about float fishing, but you must set your depth so the bait is in the coldwater zone, generally within a foot of the bottom. Pike are reluctant to leave the cold water – I can attest to this, because there have been times when I've intentionally set the depth shallower to avoid snags, always with no success. An electric thermometer is a must for defining the horizontal and vertical bounds of the cold water. But even if you find cold water from top to bottom, you'll still do better by fishing within a foot of bottom, especially for the biggest pike. Smaller ones seem more willing to chase baits higher up in the coldwater zone, but the big fish lie flat to the bottom and usually won't show up on a graph.

Coldwater pike aren't fussy about the type of baitfish – as long as it's big and lively. My usual bait is a 9- to 12-inch sucker, but I've had good luck with even bigger ones, up to 14 inches, when they're available. I've also scored with creek chubs, stonerollers, redhorse and even sheepshead that I caught on hook and line. When the bait loses its vigor, replace it. Dying or dead baits, including smelt, are seldom productive for this type of fishing.

If you plan to release your fish, I recommend a quick-strike rig. This way, when you get a bite, you can set the hook immediately and usually hook the fish in the mouth rather than the throat. I've had equally good success by pushing a 4/0 to 6/0 single hook through the baitfish's snout, then waiting for a minute or so before setting the hook. But with this method, you'll hook more fish in the gullet and risk killing them.

The best way to fish a small coldwater pocket is to double-anchor your boat from the bow and stern, crosswise to the wind. Then, you can fish several lines in the pocket without tangling. For a large pocket, try drifting through it with your lines trailing downwind, using your trolling motor to control the drift. Make several parallel drifts until you cover the entire pocket.

Some coldwater pockets may be too shallow to fish with a bobber rig. In this case, try casting to the fish with a bucktail, spinnerbait,

jerkbait or shallow running crankbait. I've even caught a few pike by casting topwaters such as buzzbaits and propbaits right into the spot where the cold water flows in. Another way to fish a shallow pocket is to toss out an unweighted minnow beneath a float.

Although float-fishing works best in deep coldwater pockets, you can also fish them with a deep-diving crankbait or a jig and minnow. I always keep the minnows that die while I'm float fishing and use them for tipping jigs.

Slide a bobber stop, a bead and a weighted 8-inch cylinder float onto your line. Add a ¾-ounce egg sinker and then tie on an 18-inch, 30-pound-test braided wire leader with a size 6/0 single hook. Push the hook through the upper jaw of a 9- to 12-inch sucker. You can also hook the sucker on a quick-strike rig.

LURES & BAITS FOR SPRING-HOLE PIKE

(1) Bucher Tandem Buzzer, (2) Harasser bucktail, (3) Suick jerkbait, (4) Slammer Thunderhead, (5) Bagley DB-06 crankbait, (6) Super Shad Rap, (7) jig and sucker, (8) Lindy Big Fin spinnerbait.

Open-water trolling is a hit-and-miss proposition, but there are some big rewards.

Deepwater Pike Tactics

Your odds of finding big deepwater pike are best in mesotrophic or oligotrophic lakes whose depths stay cool and oxygenated all year. When the shallows of these lakes get too warm, pike simply slip into deeper water. Just where in that deep water depends mainly on the type of forage. If perch are the predominant forage fish, for instance, you're likely to find the pike at depths of 40 feet or less, closely associated with structure. But if pelagic baitfish like ciscoes or smelt are the main forage, pike are less likely to associate with structure and may roam the entire lake. You'll find most of them at depths of 30 to 60 feet, but they may go as deep as 100 feet.

A few years ago, I was fishing walleyes around a 10-foot hump on a meso lake (with perch forage) in northern Minnesota. While unhooking a walleye, the wind blew my boat about 100 yards from the hump, so I cranked up the motor and started back. On the way, I glanced at my graph and noticed several big "hooks" in 35 feet of water, so I quickly lowered a jig and minnow to the bottom. I instantly felt a sharp rap, set the hook, and reeled in my line – minus the jig. "Snake," I muttered to my partner as I proceeded to tie on another jig, this time with a short wire leader. The next rap proved to be a 19-pound pike.

In a few minutes, I caught three more, the smallest being 14 pounds. Since that time, I usually make it a point to graph the deep water adjacent to good walleye spots. It's a hit-and-miss proposition, but it's paid off for me quite a few times. In fact, I keep a spare rod with a jig and wire leader in my rod box just for that purpose.

Finding deepwater pike in cisco or smelt lakes can be an even greater challenge, because you can't rely on structure to locate them. Recent research confirms that pike, walleyes and even smallmouth bass in lakes of this type spend a good deal of their time cruising open water in pursuit of suspended baitfish. Most fishermen would never think of tossing out a lure and trolling across the middle of a lake, with no regard to depth, but that may well be the best strategy in this situation.

Using a downrigger set-up or lead-line rig, start trolling while keeping a close eye on your graph. Practically any big-pike lure will work. I've got an old, jointed Pikie Minnow in my tackle box that used to be brown, but it's got so many teeth marks, it's now hard to tell what color it is. Vibrating plugs, like a Rat-L-Trap or Rattlin' Rap, are proven pike slayers, and I've had good success on a size 18 Rapala. Bucktail spinners, while considered casting lures by most anglers, also work very well for trolling. Don't use big-lipped, deep-diving plugs when trolling with downriggers; they pull so hard that they'll often trip your releases.

Try to keep the lure at the depth where you see the most baitfish activity. In most cisco

TROLLING LURES FOR DEEPWATER PIKE

(1) Inhaler bucktail, (2) Rattlin' Rap, (3) Floating Rapala, (4) Dardevle, (5) Pikie Minnow, (6) Believer.

lakes, this will be the 30- to 50-foot zone. You can easily reach 40 feet with a lead-line rig, but for deeper water, downriggers work much better. There are many other ways to get your lures deep, but these methods give you the best depth control.

Deepwater pike fishing is one of the "last frontiers" in freshwater angling. I don't know anyone who claims to be an expert at it, and very little has been written on the subject. It doesn't work everywhere; in fact, it's probably a waste of time in lakes where a 7-pound-plus pike is a rare catch. The potential is greatest in

lakes that regularly produce fish like that in spring and fall, but rarely in summer.

You've probably heard the old saying, "the fish are shallow, deep or somewhere in between." Yet the majority of pike fishermen insist on fishing shallow weedbeds even though they're catching nothing but hammer-handles. Why not try deep or somewhere in between? Probably because everything they learned from their dad, read in magazines, saw in paintings or watched on TV suggested that pike are found in shallow weeds. I guess old habits are hard to change.

TIPS FOR DOWNRIGGER TROLLING

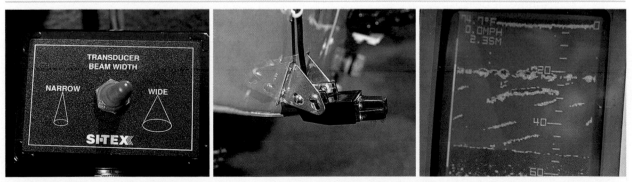

Use a transducer with a wide-angle cone for downrigger trolling. Some units (left) enable you to switch between wide and narrow cones. The face of the transducer should be angled to the rear (middle) so you can graph the downrigger balls (right). If the transducer angles forward, the balls would be out of the transducer's cone.

Catfish

These bewhiskered bruisers are finally gaining the respect they deserve.

FRESH BAITS FOR GIANT CATS

by Gerald Almy

A blood-red sun nudges its way above the cypress-rimmed horizon in the east as Bob George steers his 20-foot fishing boat in tight circles, studying his depth finder intently. Suddenly, thick marks light up the flasher. George cuts the motor and, with one deft movement, eases a huge sea anchor overboard.

We are seemingly in the middle of nowhere – miles from shore – on sprawling Santee-Cooper Lake in the lowlands of central South Carolina. But to the part-Indian guide, we are on the perfect spot to catch a giant blue catfish, or maybe even a channel or flathead.

And if anyone should know where and how to catch giant open-water cats, it's George. He has a keen knowledge of catfish habits, which he uses to put his clients on awesome numbers of big fish. Each year they pull dozens of cats in the 30- to 60-pound class, plus hundreds of 10- to 25-pounders, out of these fertile waters. The techniques George uses will produce catfish wherever they're found in large open-water areas.

"This is part of an old canal wall that the slaves built," George explains in his typical subdued manner. "It's 40 feet down but comes up about 15 feet off the bottom. Big cats love vertical structure like that."

Steaking a fresh herring he caught the day before into five chunks of fresh bait, George deftly slips each one onto a 6/0 hook. Eighteen inches above the hook is a stout swivel; above that, a 1-ounce egg sinker.

Lowering the bait to the bottom with the long baitcasting outfit, George feels the weight touch the lake floor, reels up a foot and places the rod in a holder. Five times the ritual is repeated, and before guide and angler have even had a chance to pour a cup of coffee, one of the rods bounces sharply in its holder, then bends into a deep throbbing arch.

Jumping from my seat, I grab the outfit from its holder, set the hook and feel the incredible weight and power of a huge cat bulling towards cover. There is nothing to do but hold on and hope for the best during the first few minutes as the wild cat rampages deep. But finally I gain a bit of line and work the cat near the surface. Seeing the boat, the big catfish surges back deep, stripping 30-pound line from the reel like sewing thread.

I bring the fish back to the surface again. This time George swiftly engulfs it with the mesh of the landing net. Struggling, we hoist aboard 47 pounds of sleek blue catfish.

It is a massive fish but, for George, it's just another good cat, one of countless huge fish his customers take every season. And there are others – even larger fish – that never are subdued.

"A while back, I was out with a party fishing rockfish (striped bass), but the fish weren't doing anything," George recalls. "I said to those boys, `Let's get over on some real action!' We went to one of my favorite catfish spots and I set out five lines. Before I could put out the sixth outfit, all five of those rods bent double. We never did get any of those fish. Every cat that bit broke 30-pound line."

Fortunately, not all cats tear up his tackle quite so badly. With fish capable of doing what those five cats did, however, George insists on stout gear for challenging big blues, channels and flatheads.

Gearing Up For Giant Cats

An 8- to 9-foot medium- or heavy-power graphite casting rod is ideal for big cats. "The long rod is helpful for keeping baits separated. It is also effective for pulling fish out from beneath the boat during a fight, or for keeping them away from the propeller blades," says George. "A long handle is best so the rod can fit easily in a holder and be wedged under your arm when fighting a huge cat. This latter point is particularly important, since battles with lunker catfish might last 20 minutes or more when a particularly big fish is hooked."

Use a level-wind reel with a smooth drag and spool up with 25- or 30-pound monofilament."

You'll need a seaworthy boat, 17 feet or longer, for big-water catfishing. The boat should have a deep hull, because rough weather may develop in the open-water haunts you'll be fishing. Many of the boats designed for striper fishing and inshore salt-water fishing are perfect for catfishing on large lakes. The bigger the boat, the more you can spread your rods out and cover a wide area with the baits.

The boat should be rigged with rod holders, a compass, depth finder, anchor, large cooler, fillet knife, cutting board, spare tools and terminal gear.

THE BASIC SETUP

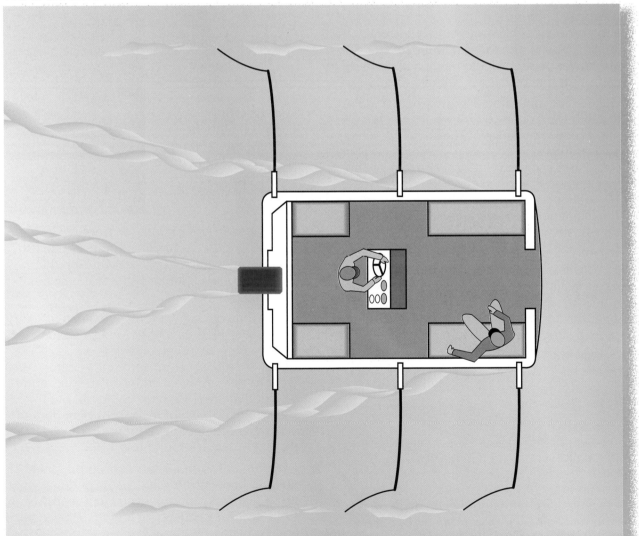

Set out about 6 rods, placing each one in a rod holder that keeps it perpendicular to the boat. The rod holders should be arranged so they are evenly spaced along both gunwales, ensuring maximum coverage and preventing constant line tangling.

Selecting The Right Bait

Another important part of George's system is fresh bait. Countless brands of commercial and homemade catfish baits are available, but George contends that nothing can top fresh, natural baits. He recommends offerings that are native to the waters you fish. They should always be as fresh as possible.

Starting in mid-February, locks on the Santee-Cooper dam near Pinopolis are opened, letting anadromous herring into the lake. These thin, silvery fish from the Atlantic can be dipped or caught with cast nets near the dam. This is George's favorite bait from midwinter through spring. Cats, especially flatheads, will take whole live herring. For blues and channels, chunking the herring into four or five steaks about three-quarters of an inch thick is best. The head also makes a good bait.

If you don't have herring in the waters you fish, try whole or cut shad. Catch them with dip nets or cast nets or snag them. Keep the bait alive or place it on ice immediately after catching it.

In summer months, catalpa worms start appearing on shoreline trees and cats feed heavily on them. Amazingly, fish up to 45 pounds will take these small offerings fished on the bottom. Freshwater mussels are another good catfish bait. But nothing equals fresh cut bait, particularly an oily variety such as herring or shad.

Make a herring rig by sliding a 1/2- to 2-ounce egg sinker onto your line (30-pound mono) and tying on a barrel swivel. To the other end of the swivel, attach a 2- to 3-foot leader of 30- to 50-pound mono, then tie on a size 4/0 to 7/0 hook. George prefers an Eagle Claw Series 42RP. Hook a herring steak through the belly, as shown.

Other Fresh Baits for Catfish

Hook a catalpa worm (above) or the firm meat of a clam (left) as shown, and fish it on a slip-sinker rig.

Finding & Fishing Giant Cats

When searching for big catfish, George stresses the importance of finding a lake that has a history of producing them. Consult state wardens and fisheries biologists and local NAFC Fishing Information Network (F.I.N.) Affiliates to ferret out these top spots for lunker cats.

Once you've selected a body of water, buy a topographic map of the lake (below) and study it to find possible catfish hangouts. Then go out in your boat, locate those spots with a depth finder and check them for fish.

In spring, big cats move into surprisingly shallow water. "I've caught them in as little as three feet of water in March and April," George said. "Other times they might be as deep as 12 feet." Long, sloping points, flats, bars, old roadbeds and shallow flooded timber all are worth prospecting for spring catfish. Anchor and cast to the area where you expect fish to be, put the rods in their holders and wait. When a fish takes the bait, give him a few seconds, then set the hook with a hard sweep of the rod.

As the water warms up in summer, look for big cats in deeper water where they seek out cooler temperatures. Shallows still can produce a flurry of action early and late in the day, but for the most part, deep water is the payoff zone for the largest summer catfish. Depths of 20 to 60 feet are optimum.

But depth is only part of the formula. "Old flooded bridges, canals, roadbeds, buildings, cemeteries, sharp dropoffs, holes, timbered bars, anything rough – that's what a big cat will hold around," George says. "They seem to like tall structure, like a wall on a flooded building or canal. When the depth finder lights up red for a 10- to 15-foot span, you're on top-notch cat cover!" A flat bottom that suddenly drops off five or ten feet into a hole is another choice spot for finding jumbo summer catfish.

Once you've located prime, deep-water catfish structure, try anchoring or drift fishing. Anchoring works best on a small, specific piece of structure, such as a flooded building or sharp drop-off. This is the best way to stay right on that cover, especially on a windy day.

Drifting works better for covering a broad area holding scattered cats. They don't hesitate to chase a bait pulled in front of them. You'll see for yourself. Giant cats are anything but lazy.

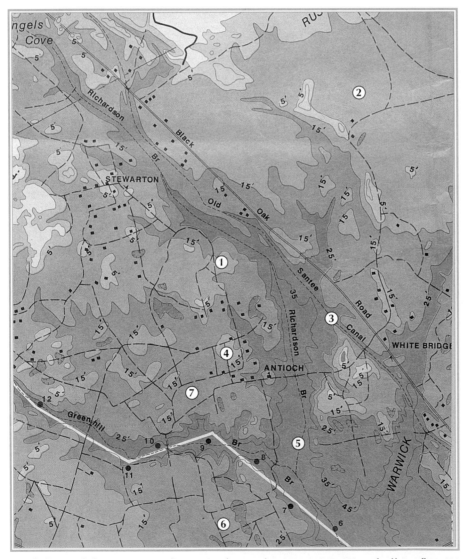

Look for catfish in spots such as (1) a long, sloping point; (2) a shallow flat; (3) a deep canal; (4) around building foundations (black squares); (5) a creek channel; (6) a deep hole and (7) an old roadbed (red line).

Know Your Cats

BLUE CATFISH. With its deeply forked tail, the blue cat bears a close resemblance to the channel cat. But the anal fin is much longer than that of a channel cat and has at least 30 rays. Blue cats have bluish to grayish sides that are not spotted.

WORLD RECORD: 111 pounds, caught in Wheeler Reservoir, Alabama, in 1996.

FLATHEAD CATFISH. Commonly called the mud cat, the flathead has mottled, brownish-yellow sides. As its name suggests, it has a flattened head, giving it a completely different look that other catfish. The tail is squarish and the lower jaw protrudes beyond the upper.

WORLD RECORD: 98 pounds, from Lake Lewisville, Texas, in 1986.

CHANNEL CAT. Often called the blue channel cat, this fish has dark bluish gray to greenish gray sides, usually with black spots. Large channel cats may not be spotted. The tail is deeply forked, and the anal fin, with 23 to 29 rays, is shorter than that of a blue cat.

WORLD RECORD: 58 pounds, taken in Santee-Cooper Reservoir, South Carolina, in 1964.

JUGGIN' SUSPENDED CATS

by Harry Ryan

I n the heat of summer, catfish seem to mysteriously disappear from most lakes and ponds. Catfish anglers have long recognized this phenomenon, but few know how to put catfish in the boat once the summer slump sets in. "I'd venture to say that virtually every catfish angler in America who floats a boat in farm ponds, small lakes and even in some impoundments, has experienced the summer slump at one time or another," says Chris Altman, an outdoor writer and catfishing authority from Pikeville, Kentucky.

"The summer slump experienced by catfish anglers is a reflection of a change in the aquatic environment that actually prevents cats from roaming a lake's depths," Altman says. This phenomenon is called thermal stratification. It is something that catfish anglers must

UNDERSTANDING
LAKE STRATIFICATION & TURNOVER

In order to understand lake stratification and turnover you must first understand the physical properties of water. Here are the key points:

•Water is densest at a temperature of 39.2 °F. As water gets warmer or colder, it becomes less dense.

•Because of this difference in density, most lakes stratify into temperature layers. The deepest, coldest, densest layer is called the hypolimnion; the shallowest, warmest, lightest layer, the epilimnion. Between the two is a zone called the thermocline, where the temperature changes rapidly.

•Just as gasoline floats on water, the warmer, lighter water in the epilimnion stays on top of the cooler, heavier water in the depths. And because the water is lighter, it is more easily circulated by the wind. The thermocline may have slight water circulation, but the water below it circulates very little, if at all.

•After a lake stratifies in early summer and water in the depths no longer mixes, a stagnation process begins. Decaying organic material on the lake bottom, along with living organisms in the water, consume dissolved oxygen. With no circulation to restore it and no aquatic plants to produce it, oxygen levels in the hypolimnion begin to decline.

•How fast the oxygen level declines depends on the water fertility. In eutrophic (highly fertile) lakes, oxygen is consumed rapidly. By midsummer, oxygen levels in the depths are too low to support gamefish, so they are forced to stay in shallow water, where contact with the air and photosynthesis by aquatic plants keeps oxygen levels high. Oxygen depletion is not a problem in oligotrophic (infertile) lakes, because there is much less decaying organic material on the bottom and far fewer living organisms in the water to consume it.

•The temperature layers remain intact through the summer, as long as the weather is warm enough to keep the surface several degrees warmer than the water in the depths. But when the weather cools enough that the shallows reach the same temperature as the depths, the fall turnover begins. Because all of the water in the lake is now at the same temperature and density, the wind can circulate the entire water mass. As the surface continues to cool, the water becomes denser than that in the depths so it sinks vertically, bolstering the mixing process.

•Mixing from top to bottom continues through the fall. Theoretically, you would expect mixing to stop when the surface cools to 39.2°F because, at that temperature, the surface water becomes lighter than the water below. But, in reality, the mixing process continues until the surface temperature reaches about 35°F, because there is very little difference in water density at these low temperatures, and strong fall winds override density differences, keeping the circulation going. In the North, the surface freezes, but the water on the bottom stays several degrees above freezing. If water did not have the unusual property of being densest at a temperature slightly above freezing, lakes would freeze completely to the bottom.

•The fall turnover takes place at different times in different lakes. A deep lake turns over later in fall than a nearby shallow lake. Because the water in the depths is colder, more time is needed for the surface water to reach the same temperature.

•A shallow, dishpan-shaped lake may never stratify or turn over, because the wind keeps the water circulating all the time.

understand and deal with to successfully fish a thermally stratified body of water.

"In the hot summer months, the thermocline (see sidebar) dictates the lower depth where cats can feed and survive," says Altman. Understanding the thermocline and why thermal stratification occurs helps the angler catch more cats during those lean summer months.

"Catfish are, for the most part, a deep-water, bottom-dwelling species, so anglers are accustomed to looking for them in deeper holes," says Altman. "But when the lake stratifies, the cats leave the deeper areas because conditions are more favorable for them in shallower water. Now anglers have to do a little detective work to find the cats."

Through the years, Altman has learned several ways to pinpoint the thermoclines. "The easiest and most convenient method is simply using your depth finder," he says. "By cranking up the sensitivity on your liquid-crystal, you can often see the thermocline. It appears as a hazy, horizontal band across the screen. A sonar unit cannot pick up water temperature changes; what you're actually seeing is the layer of plankton that commonly collects in the thermocline."

Another means of locating the 'cline is by using an electric thermometer. "These units usually have a probe that you lower on a coaxial cable marked in 1-foot increments. By dropping the probe 1 foot at a time, you can actually map the thermocline by simply watching the temperature change on the unit's meter. When the probe reaches the thermocline, the temperature drops rapidly, about half a degree per foot of depth," Altman explains. "When the probe exits the bottom of the thermocline, the temperature continues to fall, but at a much slower rate."

You can easily find the thermocline with an electric thermometer.

In the majority of good-sized lakes, the thermocline forms somewhere between 15 and 30 feet. If you don't have a graph or an electric thermometer, start at that depth range and do a little experimenting. Begin at about 30 feet and begin raise your bait 1 or 2 feet at a time until you find the cats. On smaller lakes, the thermocline is often shallower.

After pondering the effects of thermal stratification on catfish, an angler might conclude that the best strategy is to target areas of the lake bottom that are in or above the thermocline. While that approach may put cats in your livewell, Altman has learned that a high percentage of catfish do not hold or relate to any type of physical structure.

"Cats often suspend in the thermocline far from any structure," Altman says. "A lot of the cats suspend right at the top of the thermocline, lying on this water seam just as if it were the lake's bottom. The problem is that they may be anywhere in the lake, and this makes them rather difficult to locate."

They may be in the middle of the lake as well as along the shoreline, so your best bet is to use a technique that covers a great deal of water. That's why Altman recommends jug fishing, a rather primitive method by most standards but, nevertheless, a tremendously productive one. By attaching a baited hook and line to a floating jug and then releasing the rig to float away, you can cover a tremendous amount of water while keeping your bait at a precise depth. And you don't even have to be there while the jugs float across the lake, only to pick them up. "Jug fishing is, without question, the most effective technique to catch catfish in a thermally stratified body of water," Altman contends.

When the air temperature drops in early autumn, cool night temperatures cause the lake layers to begin mixing. This renews deep-water oxygen levels, effectively ending jug fishing. Autumn storms and heavy winds help speed the process, which eventually mixes the lake from top to bottom. This is known as the fall turnover. Shortly after this occurs, catfish can again be found at any depth. Often, a lake turns a dark brown color and emits a sulfurous "swamp gas" odor.

"When the turnover occurs, jugging basically goes to pot," Altman says. "The catfish typically move to deeper areas where they are beyond a jug line's reach, and they stay in the lake's deeper holes through the winter months."

Equipment for Jug Fishing

Although catfishing jugs can be made from virtually any plastic container with a screw-on cap, Altman prefers clean, 1-quart, plastic motor-oil bottles. "The problem with larger bottles, such as gallon milk jugs, is that they take up too much room in the boat," he points out. Put 40 or 50 gallon jugs in your boat and they'll blow out at the most inopportune times."

Oil jugs, on the other hand, are compact and easy to stash in your boat's livewells and dry-storage compartments. Although they are small, these 1-quart jugs will tire even a 30-pound cat.

"Jugs with screw-on caps make it easy to change the line's length," Altman says. "To shorten the line, simply push the excess into the jug, slip a loop around the threaded spout and screw the cap back on. That might not seem too secure, but the cats can't put much pressure on it because the floating jug gives them nothing to pull against."

"In larger lakes and impoundments, bigger jugs that can be seen at greater distances may be necessary," Altman advises. "Two-liter pop bottles work well, and most of them have a rim around the neck that makes a good spot for tying on the line. Because they are made of clear plastic, you should paint them a bright color to increase their visibility. It may sound strange, but I've found that white jugs are the most visible across a large expanse of water. Yellow or fluorescent orange are easily spotted, too."

"I put average-sized baits on my oil-jug rigs, but I also carry a few 2-liter pop bottles or gallon-sized milk jugs to use with big baits when I want to catch a big cat." One problem that Altman has found in using a smaller jug is that a large cat can pull it under far enough to snag the line on an underwater obstacle. If this happens, you may never find the jug or the cat you hooked.

Altman recommends using 15 to 20 jugs per angler. "That makes for an entertaining evening," he says. "Any more than that and the play turns into work."

Be sure to check local regulations on jug fishing. It's illegal in some states, others have a limit on the number of jugs allowed per

To make a catfishing jug, drill a small hole through the cap and run a piece of monofilament line through the hole. Next, tie a metal washer to the line on the inside of the lid. Screw on the lid, tie a size 1/0 or 2/0 hook to the other end of the line, and add a 1/4- to 1-ounce rubber core sinker 18 to 24 inches above the hook. Long lines or live bait require more weight than shorter lines or cut bait. When using a hand-sized bluegill or an 8-inch creek chub for bait, use hooks as large as 5/0.

angler, and many require anglers to mark each jug with a name, address and phone number.

Altman suggests marking the line length on the top of each jug. This way, you can quickly determine the depth at which most cats are feeding and then adjust the depth on your other jugs accordingly. "If you find you are catching most of your fish an an 8-foot line," he says, "then you should immediately adjust all of your lines to that length. In ponds and small lakes with a relatively shallow thermocline, 5 to 10 feet of line is usually all you need. In larger lakes, where the thermocline may form 15 to 25 feet below the surface, you need to use a longer line."

How to Jug Fish

Toss out your jugs while motoring along at a right angle to the wind. This way, each jug covers different water rather than one drifting behind the other.

ALTMAN'S FAVORITE CAT BAITS

(1) Bluegill on size 5 hook, (2) chub on size 1 hook, (3) cut shad on size 1 hook.

"I've baited my jugs with virtually everything imaginable through the years," Altman says. "On occasion, almost anything will catch catfish. My favorite bait for use on a smaller jug is a freshly trapped 4- or 5-inch creek minnow, like a sucker or chub. For large cats, I use big bluegills. The struggle of a live fish tends to attract cats. Cut bait made from shad, bluegill or even carp also works well, but it's not on a par with a live offering." Altman generally doesn't use soft baits like chicken liver and stinkbaits for jug fishing because little cats pick the hooks clean before a big cat can get to them. And big cats can steal these soft baits without getting hooked.

Jug fishing is most often done at night, because that's when catfish feed most actively. Also, floating jugs pose a very real hazard for water skiers and other boaters. Yet another reason for night fishing is that gar, if they are present, pick your baited hooks clean during the day.

Some anglers drop their jugs and check on them periodically throughout the night. But finding the jugs after dark is a challenge. Others drop their jugs around sundown and check on them early the next morning.

Wind direction obviously plays a vital role in jug fishing. You must drop the jugs on the upwind side of the lake and try to determine which direction the wind will take them. By selecting the lake's widest span, you can cover the most water with the least effort, but it may take extra time to locate all the jugs in the morning.

One of Altman's favorite jugging areas is a creek arm directly off the main lake. "I like to

Wind

find a long creek arm with a relatively deep, distinct channel running through it. Ideally, I prefer the wind to be blowing directly into the arm. When I set the jugs, I scatter them at 10- to 30-yard intervals across the creek mouth and let the wind blow them up the creek." This tactic not only lets his bait cover various depths and structure, but the jugs move into a more confined area where they are easier to find.

Nocturnal jugging requires a powerful, hand-held spotlight for locating the jugs. Altman prefers night jugging with a partner or two. "A buddy not only makes the trip a lot more enjoyable," he says, "but is a help in dropping and locating the jugs, as well as chasing down those jugs being carried away by big cats. When we start looking for jugs, one of us operates the outboard while the other sits up front, scanning the water with the spotlight for fugitive jugs and renegade cats. When we approach a jug, we kill the outboard. The person in the bow then uses a powerful electric trolling motor to close in on the jug."

"When a catfish is hooked, it usually swims away with the jug in tow. A cat of any size is difficult to run down. When you begin easing the boat near

With the wind blowing up a creek arm, set a row of jugs across the mouth of the arm, as shown. The jugs will drift up the arm, covering it thoroughly. They will then collect at the upper end, where finding them will be easy.

the jug, the cat often makes a sudden dive and pulls the jug under. Then the jug emerges a few minutes later a hundred yards or so away from the boat. On a good night, you spend most of your time chasing cats, and the sun peeks over the horizon before you know it."

When you pick up a jug, retrieve the line gently with your fingertips so you can drop it if a big cat suddenly takes off. Never wrap the jug line around your hand, Altman warns. "A big cat may not feel very heavy when you pick up the jug, but you're likely to go swimming if he makes a run and you get your hand tangled in the line."

A powerful spotlight is a must for finding jugs after dark.

INDEX

A

Altman, Chris, 147–51
Anderson, Dennis, 50

B

Bagley Bang-O-Lure for jerkin', 15
Baits. *See also* Equipment; Lures;
Rods
    for bluegill, 52–53
    for catfish, 141–44
    for coldwater pike, 135–36
    for lake trout, 103
    for night fishing, 128–29
    for northern pike, 121–23
    for striped bass, 10
    for vertical casting, 96
    for walleye, 76
Baksay, Terry, 27–31
Bass. *See* Largemouth bass;
    Smallmouth bass; Striped bass
Bishop, Dave, 7–9
Blitz Blades in vertical casting, 96
Blue catfish, 145
Bluegills, 49–53
    baits, lure, and techniques for,
        52–53
    ice fishing for, 44–45
    locating, 51
    researching, 49–50
    sedentary nature of, 50–51
    spawning habits of, 49, 50
Boat control in night fishing, 129
Bohn, Greg, 87–91
Bomber Long A for jerkin', 15
Bridge piers, fishing for striped
    bass near, 8, 9
Broadleaf cabbage, 88, 90
Bucktail jigs
    for lake trout, 103
    for muskies, 125
    in night fishing, 128–29
Bull gill. *See* Bluegill
Burcher, Joe, 124–29

C

Canada waterweed, 88, 89
Catalpa worms in catfish
    fishing, 143
Catfish
    baits for, 141–44
    equipment for, 142
    locating, 144
    summer fishing for, 147–51
    types of, 145
Channel catfish, 145

Chara, 89
Chenille-and-marabou jigs in
    crappie fishing, 38–39
Cannulae, Bob, 107–11
Cold front
    largemouth bass fishing
        during, 13
    muskie fishing during, 126
Coldwater pike
    fishing coldwater pockets
        for, 134–35
    sources for, 133
    summer fishing for, 130–37
    tactics for deep-water, 136–37
    tips for finding, 133
Coldwater pockets, fishing, 134–35
Conservation measures for
    tournament fishing, 24
Coontail, 89
Crankbaits
    in night fishing, 129
    in walleye fishing, 76, 78
Crappies, 35–39
    equipment, lures, and techniques
        for fishing, 38–39
    in fall fishing, 37
    ice fishing for, 41–43
    in summer fishing, 35, 36–37
Cumberland River, striped bass
    fishing in, 11
Curlytail jigs
    in crappie fishing, 39
    in walleye fishing, 59
Currents
    coping with Great Lakes, 107–11
    impact on fishing, 108–9
Cutbait, tipping jigs with, 104
Cyalume light stick, in night
    fishing, 43

D

Dale Hollow Reservoir, smallmouth
    bass fishing in, 19
Dams
    fishing for striped bass near, 7
    oxygen problems near, 7
Dead-stickin', 47
Dead zone, 65
Dean, Emil, 113–17
Deep jigging for winter lake
    trout, 101–6
Deep-water lakers, vertical
    casting for, 94–99
Depth control in walleye fishing, 74
Depth finder
    in locating schools of
        crappies, 36–37
    in night fishing, 128
    in walleye fishing, 65

Devil's Lake, yellow perch
    fishing in, 46
Diedrich, Bill, 94–99
Do-Jigger Spoon in yellow perch
    fishing, 47
Downriggers, stacking
    spoons on, 110
Downrigger trolling, 137
Drift and twitch technique for
    largemouth bass, 28–31
Drop-back technique for river
    steelhead, 113–17

E

Eagle Claw hook in striped bass
    fishing, 10
Electronics
    in lake trout fishing, 102
    in walleye fishing, 65
Elodea, 89
Equipment. *See also* Baits;
Electronics; Lures; Rods
    in crappie fishing, 38–39
    in jug fishing, 149
    in smallmouth bass
        fishing, 20–22
Eriquez, Doug, 35–39

F

Fall, finding crappies in, 37
Fall turnover, 148
Farm pond fishing, 50
Feather jigs, for lake trout, 103
Fishing techniques
    for bluegills, 52–53
    for crappies, 38–39
    for largemouth bass,
        16–17, 28–31
    for night fishing, 128–29
    for steelhead, 113–17
    for striped bass, 11
    for vertical casting, 96–99
    for walleye, 82, 84–85
Flathead catfish, 145
Flats
    cover for, 14
    jerkin' for largemouth
        bass, 13–17
    locating, 14
    slope of, 14
Fluctuating water levels in walleye
    fishing, 60
Fluorescent mono in night
    fishing, 20
Fly 'n rind in night fishing,
    21, 22, 23

Funk, Dave, 98
Fuzz-E-Grub in crappie fishing, 39

G

George, Bob, 141–44
**Gizzard shad in striped bass
    fishing,** 10
GPS
    in vertical casting, 96
    in walleye fishing, 79
**Great Lakes currents, coping
    with,** 107–11
Grzywinski, Dick, 63–67, 81–85

H

Hair jigs in night fishing, 22
Hale's Craw Worm, 22
Headlamps in night fishing, 128
Heddon Sonar
    for lake trout, 103
    in vertical casting, 96
Herring
    in catfish fishing, 143
    in striped bass fishing, 10
Holt, Steven, 74
Hoot-N-Ninny, 22
**Hudson River, largemouth bass
    fishing in,** 27
Humps, night fishing near, 23
Hydrographic maps, 42, 67, 90

I

Ice fishing, 41–47
    bluegills in, 44–45
    crappies in, 41–43
    Northern Pike in, 121–23
    walleyes in, 69–71
    yellow perch in, 46–47
Ice-out
    and fishing for early-season
        walleyes, 63
    and fishing for largemouth
        bass, 14
**Impoundment tributaries, large-
    mouth bass fishing in,** 27
**Indentations in breaklines, in
    walleye fishing,** 67
In-line planer, 73

J

Jerking minnowbaits, 14
**Jerkin' the flats for largemouth
    bass,** 13–17
    lures and equipment for, 15
    techniques in, 16–17
Jigging
    for bluegill, 45
    for crappies, 39, 42–43
    for lake trout, 104–5
    in night fishing, 21, 22
    for northern pike, 121
    for walleyes, 58–61, 69–71
Jitterbugs in night fishing, 21
Jug fishing
    equipment for, 149
    strategies for, 150–51
    wind direction in, 150

K

Kelso, Arthur, Jr., 7–11

L

**Lake Huron, yellow perch
    fishing in,** 46
**Lake James Chain, fishing for
    largemouth bass in,** 13
Lake Pepin, coldwater pike in, 130
Lakes
    **finding open-water
        crappies in,** 35–39
    **finding sleeper, for
        bluegill,** 44–45
    **stratification and turnover
        in,** 147
**Lake Sakakawea, walleye
    fishing in,** 85
**Lake Simcoe, yellow perch
    fishing in,** 46
Lake trout
    baits and lures for, 103
    coldwater habits of, 101
    deep jigging for winter, 101–6
    electronics in fishing for, 102
    jigging for, 104–5
    vertical casting for deep-
        water, 94–99
**Lake Winnebago, walleye
    fishing in,** 72
**Lake Winnibigoshish, walleye
    fishing in,** 81
Largemouth bass
    drift and twitch technique
        for, 28–31

effect of cold front on fishing
    for, 13
jerkin' the flats for, 13–17
surface fishing for, 27–31
topwater fishing for, 14, 27
**Leech Lake, yellow perch
    fishing in,** 46
Lehrman, Art, 56, 60, 61
Lincoln, Dave, 56–61
**Livewell, cooling water in, during
    hot weather,** 24
**Luhr-Jensen Krocodiles in vertical
    casting,** 96
**Luhr-Jensen Ripple Tail for
    lake trout,** 103
Lures. *See also* Baits; Equipment;
Rods
    for bluegill, 52–53
    for coldwater pike, 135
    for crappies, 38–39
    for lake trout, 103
    for largemouth bass, 31
    for smallmouth bass, 20–22

M

Matching the hatch, 58
**Mayfly wiggler in yellow perch
    fishing,** 47
McClintock, Fred, 19–25
Mille Lacs Lake
    walleye fishing in, 64
    yellow perch fishing in, 46
Minnows
    technique for jerking, 16
    for walleye fishing, 69–70
    weighting, 17
**Mississippi River, walleye
    fishing in,** 56, 60
Mudlines in walleye fishing, 67
Murray, Jeff, 49–53
Muskies, night fishing for, 124–29
Mussels, in catfish fishing, 143

N

**Niagara River, salmon
    fishing in,** 107
Night fishing
    Cyalume light stick in, 43
    equipment and techniques
        for, 128–29
    fluorescent mono in, 20
    jug fishing in, 151
    for muskies, 124–29
    near weedbeds, 23
    preplanning, 19

proper depth in, 19
for smallmouth bass, 19–24
spinnerbaits in, 21, 24
Northern pike
dead bait for, 121–23
jigging for, 121
tip-up fishing for, 122–23
Northland Fireball jig in walleye fishing, 85

O

Ohio River, largemouth bass fishing in, 14
Open-water trolling, 76

P

Parsons, Gary, 72, 74–79
Perch. *See* Yellow perch
Pike. *See* Coldwater pike; Northern pike
Planer boards
rigging and fishing, 75
strategies with, 78–79
types of, 73
in walleye fishing, 72–79
Plankton in crappie fishing, 36
Polar Tip-up, for northern pike, 122
Power auger in walleye fishing, 70
Precision trolling, 74
Pre-weighted baits, fine-tuning, 17

Q

Quickset Rig for northern pike, 121

R

Rapala
in crappie fishing, 39, 42
in jerkin', 13, 15
in largemouth bass fishing, 30, 31
in yellow perch fishing, 47
Rebel Spoonbill for jerkin', 15
Reservoirs, fishing for striped bass in, 7
Rip-jigging in walleye fishing, 81–85
sites for, 83
technique in, 82, 84–85
River herring in striped bass fishing, 10
Rivers
secret to successful fishing in, 57

striped bass fishing in, 7–9
walleye fishing in, 56–61
Rods. *See also* Baits; Equipment; Lures
in bluegill fishing, 52
in largemouth bass fishing, 30
in smallmouth bass fishing, 20
in walleye fishing, 89

S

Sacramento River, largemouth bass fishing in, 27
Saganaga Lake, lake trout fishing in, 98
Saginaw Bay, yellow perch fishing in, 46
Saint John's River, largemouth bass fishing in, 27
Salmon fishing
in Great Lakes, 107–11
slicks in, 108
trolling strategies in, 110–11
Sand grass, 89
Santee-Cooper Lake, fishing for catfish in, 141
Schneider, Jack, 98
Scuds in bluegill fishing, 52–53
Selwyn Lake, fishing on, 94–95
Shad bodies in walleye fishing, 59
Shodeen, Duane, 44–45
Shrimp for bluegill, 52–53
Skipjack in striped bass fishing, 10
Ski-type planer, 73
Skunkgrass, 89
Slicks in salmon fishing, 108
Slip-bobber rigs
in crappie fishing, 43
in walleye fishing, 90
Slip-sinker rigs in striped bass fishing, 10
Slug-Go in largemouth bass fishing, 30–31
Smallmouth bass
conservation measures for tournament fishing, 24
equipment and lures for, 20–22
feeding patterns for, 19
night fishing for, 19–24
spinnerbaits in, 24
Snap-jigging, 81
Snap weights in walleye fishing, 77, 78
Spider jigs in night fishing, 22, 23
Spinnerbaits in night fishing, 21, 24, 128–29
Spirit Lake, yellow perch fishing in, 46

Spoons
in salmon fishing, 110–11
stacking, on downriggers, 110
Steelhead
drop-back technique for river, 113–17
fishing conditions for, 114–16
spawning cycle of, 113
Stickbaits in largemouth bass fishing, 30–31
Stinger hooks in walleye fishing, 58
Striped bass, 7
bait and tackle for, 10
fishing for
near bridge piers, 8, 9
near dams, 7
near submerged stumps, 8, 9
near surface boils, 8–9
in reservoirs, 7
in rivers, 7–9
fishing techniques for, 11
keeping quiet while fishing for, 11
preference for cool waters, 9
topwater fishing for, 11
Submerged bank protection in walleye fishing, 57, 60
Submerged stumps, fishing for striped bass near, 8, 9
Summer
finding crappies in, 36–37
fishing for catfish in, 147–51
fishing for pike in, 130–37
fishing weeds in, for walleye, 90–91
Summer crappies, 35
Surface baits in night fishing, 128
Surface boils
fishing for striped bass near, 8–9
vertical casting near, 97
Surface fishing for largemouth bass, 27–31
Swedish hook in rigging dead baitfish, 121
Swedish Pimple
for lake trout, 103
in vertical casting, 96
in yellow perch fishing, 47

T

Tackle for bluegill, 52–53
Tailrace areas, fishing for striped bass in, 7
Thermocline, locating, in catfish fishing, 148
Three-way rigs in walleye fishing, 60, 61

Tip-up fishing for northern pike, 122–23
Topwater fishing
for largemouth bass, 14, 27
at night, 128
for striped bass, 11
Tor-P-Do spoons in vertical casting, 96–97
Tournament fishing, conservation measures for, 24
Trolling, 72
downrigger, 137
open-water, 76
precision, 74
strategies in, 110–11
Trout. *See* Lake trout
Tube jigs in crappie fishing, 39

U

Uni-knot splice, 102

V

Vertical casting
baits for, 96
for deep-water lakers, 94–99
technique in, 96–99

W

Wallace, Gord, 95, 96
Walleye fishing
bait selection in, 76
depth control in, 74, 77
early-season, 63–67
electronics in, 65
fishing weeds for, 87–91
fluctuating water levels in, 60
ice fishing for, 69–71
indentations in breaklines in, 67
jig fishing techniques for, 58–61
jigging for hardwater, 69–71
mudlines in, 67
planer board strategies in, 78–79
planing for, 72–79
playing the wind in, 66–67
rip-jigging for, 81–85
sites for, 83
technique in, 82, 84–85
river fishing for, 56–61
rods in, 89
spawning habits of, 63
submerged bank protection in, 57, 60
three-ways rigs in, 60, 61

Water clarity as issue in muskie fishing, 126
Watts Bar Lake, striped bass in, 7
Weedbeds
fishing, for walleyes, 87–91
night fishing near, 23
Williams, Larry, 13, 14–17
Wind
direction of, in jug fishing, 150
effect of, on early-season water temperature, 8/
significance of, in walleye fishing, 66–67
Windward shore in walleye fishing, 66–67
Wing dams
fishing, 61
and need for precise boat control, 60
Winnibigoshish Lake, yellow perch fishing in, 46

Y

Yellow perch, ice fishing for, 46–47
Yellowtail (threadfin) shad in striped bass fishing, 10

Z

Zara Spook in largemouth bass fishing, 30